THE
B2B
EXECUTIVE
PLAYBOOK

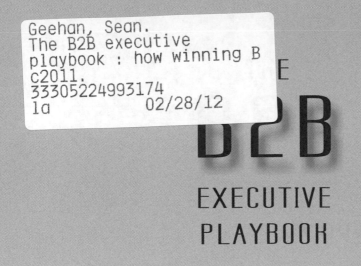

B2B

EXECUTIVE
PLAYBOOK

The Ultimate Weapon for Achieving
Sustainable, Predictable &
Profitable Growth

Sean Geehan

Founder, The Geehan Group

CLERISY PRESS

THE B2B EXECUTIVE PLAYBOOK

For further information, contact the publisher:
Clerisy Press
P.O. Box 8874
Cincinnati, OH 45208-0874
clerisypress.com

Library of Congress Cataloging-in-Publication Data:
Geehan, Sean.
    The B2B executive playbook : the ultimate weapon for achieving sustainable, predictable & profitable growth / Sean Geehan.
        p. cm.
    ISBN-13: 978-1-57860-446-3
    ISBN-10: 1-57860-446-X
    1. Industrial marketing. 2. Executives. 3. Customer relations. I. Title.
    HF5415.1263.G44 2011
    658.8'04—dc23
                        2011034195

Distributed by Publishers Group West
All images courtesy of The Geehan Group unless otherwise noted.

This book is dedicated to my parents Elmer and Maureen Geehan . . .

the two most influential people in my life.

You are the Greatest, and I love you very much!

CONTENTS

FOREWORD

Nothing is more important to me than the success of my growth company's clients, students, and friends. I have had the privilege of knowing and working with Sean Geehan for the many years he has spent advising and problem-solving with leading B2B companies.

It is incredibly difficult to define the key criteria to help B2B companies develop a consistent, profitable growth plan. Sean's *B2B Executive Playbook* succeeds with this insightful set of rules and programs that drive long-term growth. This is particularly important for B2B companies where a handful of customers account for the majority of their market and sales opportunities. *The B2B Executive Playbook* can help B2B leaders take their organizations to the top, thriving in the face of incredible competition for customer relationships.

Today's uncertain economic times require B2B companies to focus on the one constant that defines success: sales growth. Regardless of the size of business or industry, being strategically close to your customers is a prerequisite for attaining industry leadership for the next cycle. This prerequisite includes product and service innovation, market positioning and acquisitions, as well as internal alignment, prioritization, and resource allocation.

My research into growth companies reveals that achieving consistent sales growth is the hallmark of only 5 percent of management teams—and consequently, the most difficult objective for virtually all B2B teams.

With the next growth cycle about to emerge, leading companies will be defined as those achieving sales growth driven by deep customer relationships, particularly challenging for B2B companies considering the dependence on a few customers for growth. B2B customers are an extension of your management team's ability to help define your company's higher-order benefits—i.e., strategy, organizational alignment, and innovation.

More than just an overview of principles, *The B2B Executive Playbook* provides the tools and approaches that any B2B leader can apply to create huge impact with market and organizational alignment.

Sean has done a wonderful job of illustrating what works and describing why it works. He has not only analyzed winning approaches, he also has successfully tested and applied his *B2B Executive Playbook* to different B2B situations to ensure its programs and rules apply, in turn helping these companies build win-win, long-term market relationships and gain insight that ignites sustainable and profitable growth.

The real value of this book is more than its interesting case studies, programs, and rules. The real value lies in what we do with what we learn.

David G. Thomson

David G. Thomson is a world-renowned business growth consultant, keynote speaker, and best-selling author. He is the founder and chairman of the Blueprint Growth Institute, a specialized consulting firm that advises growth companies. Thomson's book, *Blueprint to a Billion*, has been translated worldwide and featured on top media globally.

INTRODUCTION

Back in the day, I was the head coach of the University of Dayton's men's water polo team. It was a young program, and in my first few years as coach, we consistently posted losing seasons. Actually, we got slaughtered. I'll never forget the televised match against the nationally ranked University of Kentucky team, in particular. By half-time, Kentucky led 14-0, which means they scored 14 goals since each is only worth one point. Kentucky's coach then played his B team the entire second half, and we still ended up losing 24-3. Ouch!

I accepted our losses because I understood it would take some time to develop the program. But I really didn't expect to fare so poorly because I had followed the conventional wisdom of water polo success: recruit big, fast swimmers and teach them how to play the game. This strategy seemed to work for other teams; it had to work for ours. So, I stayed the course and recruited even bigger and faster players and swam them even more…that's right, nobody was going to beat us down the pool. And, we continued losing.

After a couple of seasons, we headed to Southern California, the Mecca of water polo, seeking to prove we could hold our own against the best of the best. We played top-ranked Pepperdine and lost 14-1. In fact, we lost every one of the seven games we played on that humbling road trip. It was obvious we just weren't improving or even close to being competitive at a national level. I finally realized I just did not have the right formula for success. For us to be great, I needed a completely new approach.

I decided to become a better student of the game to see if there were important elements or attributes of winning water polo our team was missing or didn't understand. In my study, I learned that size and speed were not nearly as important as conventional wisdom dictated. Instead, other aspects of the game had larger impacts on the final score, including field position, minimizing your turnovers and capitalizing on those of your opponents, and understanding how to adjust your play to the refereeing. With this insight, I developed a new game plan and playbook, and enlisted experts in the sport, including the icon of U.S. water polo, five-time Olympic coach Monte Nitzkowski, to review and critique it.

After a few years of developing the team under the new strategy, we qualified for our first Collegiate National Championship tournament in 1994, and for three more over the next four years. In each tournament, we arrived with a group of players whose combined water polo experience was significantly dwarfed by each of our potential opponents, including long-time powerhouses Michigan, Florida, Texas, Michigan State, UC—Riverside, Arizona, Cal Poly, and the US Military Academy at West Point. On paper, we were clearly outmatched in terms of size, speed, and experience, but with preparation and a solid playbook, over the last five years of coaching, the Dayton team posted an enviable record of 112-6 and clinched the National Championship Title in 1995, the University of Dayton's first national sports title in 15 years. Having the right game plan and playbook clearly delivered sustainable, predictable, and successful results.

Over the past 25 years of working with business-to-business (B2B) companies, I have often felt like I was reliving my unsuccessful early days as a water polo coach. As the always quotable Yogi Berra said, it was "déjà vu all over again." The B2B company leaders, like the Dayton players and coaching staff, were smart, committed, passionate, and knowledgeable about their respective industries, but they often lacked insight into the true key fundamentals of the game they were playing.

Instead, they have developed their strategies based on conventional wisdom about business success that is often not applicable to B2B companies. I have seen this approach yield unpredictable and typically disappointing results. The 24-3 loss to Kentucky still stuck in my mind is their failed product launch, botched marketing campaign, misguided acquisition, or other equally ineffective strategy or tactic.

B2B leaders need the same thing I needed as a head coach at Dayton. They need a fresh look at the fundamentals of the game and a new playbook. I wrote this book to provide both. With the invaluable assistance and insight of my colleagues at the Geehan Group, along with a select group of our firm's clients and other market-leading B2B firms, I developed the *The B2B Executive Playbook* specifically to help B2B leaders, whether they are responsible for an entire company, a business unit, or a function, such as finance, sales, R&D, marketing, strategy, or customer service.

Why Just B2B?

Two of the best, most influential, and closely studied business books written are Jim Collins's *Good to Great* and David Thomson's *Blueprint to a Billion.* Both offer extremely valuable insight into how companies become wildly successful. Nonetheless, these and many other good business books don't distinguish between B2C (business-to-consumer) and B2B companies. In fact, of the 11 companies profiled in *Good to Great,* only one is a pure B2B company. Granted, some business issues can be similarly addressed in both types of companies. (Every leader should read *Good to Great* on "getting the right people on the bus" and *Blueprint* for advice on management-team structure). But in other critical areas, B2C and B2B companies require vastly different approaches, and these areas are major factors in B2B success on which I will focus.

In the pages ahead, you won't read about the strategies of Apple Computer or Coca-Cola or Starbucks or Disney. I know these are the companies everyone points to when they talk about business success, but they operate in the B2C realm of retailers, such as Lowe's, Kroger, and McDonalds, and consumer-package-goods manufacturers, such as PepsiCo, Procter & Gamble, and Kellogg. This world is not the same as the B2B world. Although their examples can be useful in some ways, too often what makes these B2C companies soar will stall or even stop B2B companies.

Take marketing, for example. Marketing is very different in the B2B and B2C sectors. Unlike B2C companies, B2B companies don't win customers with a Super Bowl ad, or a big following on Twitter, or a guest spot on Oprah. Nor will a celebrity spokesperson like Brett Favre, Snoop Dogg, or that cute little green gecko drive B2B success. Unfortunately, however, a significant number of well-meaning B2B executives try to apply B2C marketing strategies such as these in their companies, often with poor, and sometimes even disastrous, results.

Are You Using the Wrong Playbook?

The symptoms or pains felt by a B2B company following the wrong playbook are not new or necessarily unique. In fact, many are the same age-old business problems felt by many types of organizations. They just might be feeling new or heightened in your company due to lightning-fast changes in technology, shifts in global forces, the emergence of radically transformational business models, or other industry disruptions. These and other realities of the business environment have simply raised the risk of using the wrong playbook and are accelerating the need for adaptive change. B2B leaders know very well there is less room for error than ever before.

To know if you and your company might be using the wrong playbook, ask if:

- Your company has lost or is at risk of losing its top customers

- Margins are threatened or eroding

- New products are falling short of their revenue, margin, or market-share targets

- The relationships with the real decision makers at your most important customers are poorly developed

- Your strategic planning process is unproductive or frustrating

- Branding and marketing initiatives have fallen flat

- Your senior executive team disagrees on how to move the company forward

- Your organization confuses activities with results

These are just some of the problems that frustrate and confound many executives in B2B companies. But I've often found they aren't the real issues; they are merely symptoms of a deeper problem which is the widespread misconception that all business pains can be successfully resolved with generic business cures. As a result, B2B executives take the lessons they learn from the B2C world, whether from experience or education, and attempt to apply them to their B2B company. As most discover, this approach simply fails.

That's the bad news. The good news is that success in the B2B arena is not an overly complex undertaking. And, in almost every instance, the playbook of proven B2B strategies costs less to develop and execute than you might think—and will generate significant and measurable returns. That's the promise I'm making in this book: You can yield market-leading results while simplifying your tactics, reducing the number and cost of activities, leveraging your time and resources, and achieving greater clarity and focus.

B2B's Ultimate Weapon

The core element in *The B2B Executive Playbook*—and the ultimate strategic weapon in the B2B arsenal—is the engagement, collaboration, and advocacy of your customer decision makers. I know you've heard this before, but I'm not talking about the end-users of the products and services your company sells, or the buyers in the purchasing department. I'm talking about the handful of executives and influencers within your most valuable customer companies who ultimately determine your success help you achieve sustainable, predictable, profitable growth (SPPG).

If your company is like most B2B companies, it relegates its relationships with these key executive customers to the sales or marketing function. As a result, executive customers either get treated like sales prospects or get bombarded with marketing materials and event invitations they don't have time to read, let alone act upon. They don't find value in these interactions—just as you don't when your customers treat you in this same way. Naturally, they put up barriers to access. So now, in the time-honored tradition of treating symptoms rather than root causes, you can find a growing shelf of sales and marketing books on how to "break into" the C-suites of prospective customer companies.

You don't need to "break into" the C-suite to reach your executive customers. In fact, the true decision makers will happily come to you…if you make a place for them at the right level of your organization and engage them in strategic discussions which offer their companies real business value. This is exactly what happened for $3.3 billion Noida, India-based HCL. Up to 2008, HCL had no systemic way of interacting with the decision makers from their customers (CIOs). HCL's Americas President Shami Khorana shares, "This platform has allowed us to have an exchange of ideas with the true decision makers from our major clients to gain 'collective feedback.' This has ultimately contributed to our sales growth and the value of the services we provide." When you engage executives in a relevant way, it not only gives you ongoing access, but they are actually enthusiastic supporters. Khorana added, "These are real executives with both business acumen and extensive domain knowledge. This combination has delivered an incredible level of thought, insight, and guidance." Since launching their program, HCL hasn't lost one of their "top 80" clients involved in these programs. These clients collectively represent more than $2 billion of the $3.3 billion in total sales.

So, if and when you do decide to move forward, you will quickly discover that this small group of executive customers has the power to consistently and successfully:

- Drive alignment of your leadership team, and ultimately your entire organization with the market by developing a clear and focused strategy.

- Leverage the time and effort of your leadership team, as well as company resources.

- Deliver sustainable, predictable, profitable growth, which I will demonstrate is the true aim for any company.

I will also show how by rebalancing discretionary investments, your efforts will yield a measurable ROI on B2B specific initiatives. Imagine what that would do for your company—and your career.

I understand that this may sound like hyperbole, but I hope you'll bear with me and read on. In the pages ahead, you will see how a wide variety of B2B companies have achieved all of these benefits. Their annual revenues range from under $50 million, such as at Intesource, Inc., a boutique provider of cutting-edge procurement services and solutions, to more than $40 billion, such as at Oracle, the broad-based enterprise computing giant. The highlighted companies hail from a wide variety of industries around the globe, including information technology, health care, publishing, broadcasting, banking, legal, and foodservice equipment, among others. Furthermore, their customers include a veritable Who's Who of global business. I sought permission to include these real-life examples to prove not only are the three benefits attainable, but also that any kind of B2B company can attain them.

Coming Attractions

Before we begin, I'd like to give you an overview of the book's contents.

Chapter 1: Setting the Stage is a brief introduction to the outcome that all B2B companies should be focused on and striving towards: sustainable, predictable, profitable growth (SPPG). As the acronym SPPG suggests, each of those words is equally important. In fact, if any one of them is missing, B2B success will be fleeting at best. It's worth noting that SPPG is as important in the B2C sector as in the B2B sector. The difference between the two is how SPPG is achieved.

Chapter 2: A Different Game explores the primary differentiating factors between the B2B and B2C worlds. This chapter explains how three indisputable realities about customers define the B2B world and control the fate of the companies that operate within it.

Chapter 3: Six Benefits, Four Steps explores the core benefits of engaging your company's executive customers. It also introduces the four steps in *The B2B Executive Playbook* which can generate SPPG. Each of the steps is detailed in the four chapters that follow.

Chapter 4: Engage describes the first step on the path to SPPG. It explains how to assemble and connect your company with a market collective—that is, a select group of the key executive customers in your market. This chapter discusses how to leverage executive customers to gain a view of their industries and key markets through their eyes, as well as how to work with them to brainstorm and validate new ideas. This level of engagement increases their loyalty to your company, as opposed to the people in your company with whom they usually work.

Chapter 5: Plan describes how the market collective can build consensus among the members of your leadership team and help ensure that your strategy is properly aligned to the needs and direction of the market. It shows how the engagement of executive customers adds direction, clarity, and confidence to the strategic planning process. This chapter also reveals how your leadership team can raise the effectiveness of its M&A deals, boost new product success, rethink business models, and develop more powerful marketing, service, and sales programs.

Chapter 6: Collaborate examines how to use individual executive customer relationships to unleash innovation and build your business. It shows how leading B2B companies are driving innovation by collaborating and co-designing the next generation of offerings with executive customers. Executive customers are the most reliable sources of input throughout all the phases of the development process, including ideation, validation, testing, and adoption. They not only assure the success of new products and services by ensuring they are properly aligned with the market, they are also the best and most enthusiastic customers for these solutions.

Chapter 7: Grow unveils the final step on the path to SPPG. It shows how executive customers can become your best marketers and salespeople. This chapter describes a variety of ways in which they can act as powerful advocates to accelerate your sales cycle, enhance your margins, and build your corporate reputation, brand equity, or reposition your firm.

Chapter 8: Implementing the Playbook and *Chapter 9: Avoiding the Four Pitfalls* contain hard-won knowledge from the companies who have adopted and implemented executive customer programs. Chapter 8 describes what companies can expect as they implement executive customer programs and the roles that various members of the B2B leadership team should play to ensure success. Chapter 9 describes the most common implementation pitfalls, in the hope that they can be avoided in the future.

Your Success Starts Here

Executive customer programs are powerful strategic tools with applications that range far beyond sales and marketing. When they are sponsored and supported by the entire leadership team, they can transform the performance of B2B companies, enabling them to operate more effectively in the short-term, and more importantly, grow and profit in the long-term. Executive customer programs can drive internal and market alignment, unleash successful innovation, and differentiate you from your competitors. They leverage executive time and resources, allowing company leaders to address strategic issues and avoid getting caught up in company politics, day-to-day problems, and tactical activities. Finally, executive customer programs can help you generate sustainable, predictable, profitable growth—which, in the end, is the only metric that really matters in corporate and career success.

CHAPTER 1

SETTING THE STAGE

ACTIVATING THE B2B ULTIMATE WEAPON
TO CAPTURE SUSTAINABLE, PREDICTABLE,
PROFITABLE GROWTH

Of the most admired publicly held companies in the world, only an elite few merit the coveted title "Wall Street darling." These are the companies whose leaders have shepherded them to extraordinary runs of success, and whose corresponding stock price climbs quarter after quarter, year after year. Jack Welch and General Electric had such a run from 1981 to 2001, and its stock price rose from $1.50 to $40 on an adjusted basis. So did Larry Ellison and Oracle. From 1990 to 2011, Oracle's stock price rose from 25 cents to $33. Mark Hurd led similar runs at NCR from 2002 to 2005, where the stock price rose from $9 to $39, and then again at Hewlett-Packard from 2005 to 2010, where the stock rose from $28 to $46.

To become rock stars of commerce, these leaders put into action a formula that achieved sustainable, predictable, profitable growth (SPPG), the four words that describe the Holy Grail of business. Their companies were valued accordingly by the financial markets, and their careers took off.

For most executives, however, achieving SPPG is as elusive as the Grail itself. How close—or how far—they come to leading their organization to SPPG determines their true personal performance and legacy. How do you determine where you are on this trajectory? Take a look inside your organization at the SPPG leading indicators:

- What does the company's top and bottom line performance look like? Are both revenue and profits rising?

- What about balance sheet valuation, cash flow, and shareholder/owner equity?

If your company does not have positive measurements in all of these consistently over time, it is highly likely there are flaws in your strategic playbook.

I admit these are very basic metrics. But it is amazing how often B2B leaders get lost on their way to the end game. They get bogged down in the trends du jour—hot topics such as brand equity, change management, leadership styles, CRM, cloud computing, and social media—and they lose sight of what's really important: the timeless grail of sustainable, predictable, profitable growth.

That's why the first step in B2B success is a clear and unwavering vision of the outcome every company is striving to achieve. Whether your company is a publicly traded multinational, a venture-backed start-up with IPO aspirations, or a privately held company seeking the next level of success, SPPG should be the goal of your strategic playbook.

Profitable Growth...

It is obvious that turning a profit is a must for any company, and owners expect profits to grow year over year. In booming economies and markets, profits aren't all that difficult to capture. You keep the shelves stocked and fill the orders. But what happens when prices get driven down because the economic cycle heads south, market growth stagnates, or the competition heats up? How do you grow profits when top-line growth stalls or worse, turns negative?

Typically, profits without revenue growth come from cost-cutting initiatives. These activities are often necessary to stabilize a company and bring operating costs back into line, and they can deliver the profits owners demand in the short-term. But over the medium and long-term, these savings cannot support a company, especially one that aspires to grow and lead its industry. Without profit growth, from where will the capital come to fuel growth activities, such as research and development, account development, expansion into new markets, and strategic acquisitions? How will efforts to combat falling prices and enhance profitability, such as staving off competitors and battling commoditization, be funded?

It's clear a company cannot cut its way to greatness. At some point, the cuts bite through the fat and into muscle, and begin to hamstring the company. In fact, research shows that downturns are the right time to boost investment levels. David Thomson's Blueprint Institute found that companies that invest for growth during downturns outperform companies that hunker down until the economic cycle recovers.

To grow, a company must generate the necessary extra cash through top-line growth. But, is all top-line revenue growth worth pursuing? That depends on the margin you earn from what you sell. It is commonplace for companies to pursue any and all sales, especially during downturns ("Get deals in the door!") without fully calculating:

1. All costs to fulfill the contract, including on-boarding new clients and assimilating them into the organization.

2. The margin needed to provide a return large enough to cover the cost of capital, plus the measure of profit necessary to fuel investment and compensate owners.

3. The opportunity cost of diverting resources to fulfill contracts with low economic value, leaving none to perform activities that can be sold at a higher value.

For example, some B2B services companies chase short-term contracts, while others pursue long-term assignments that enable them to leverage their staffing and sales costs over time. Likewise, some product engineering firms chase assignments for feature and function enhancements on existing products, while others focus on customers who are making large-scale investments in products capable of transforming markets and industries.

We've worked with both types of companies, those that can't seem to help chasing every incremental dollar to boost their short-term results, and those who understand that enduring success requires a dedicated focus on long-term, large-scale revenue growth. The latter companies live by the credo that revenue quality is just as important as revenue quantity. Inevitably, they are companies that flourish or get acquired at premium valuation. Meanwhile, the former companies are still shuffling their organizational charts and slashing budgets.

So that is the first half of the SPPG story: profits must come from revenue growth, and growth must be profitable.

...That Is Sustainable and Predictable

The second half of the SPPG story is where Wall Street darlings start to pull away from the also-rans. Value investors like Warren Buffett search for profitable growth that is consistently delivered over time—that is sustainable and predictable. For example, they look for companies whose innovative products command a premium in the marketplace and are protected by patents or other barriers that stifle competition and yield attractive margins. Predictability and sustainability are growth attributes that engender analyst confidence, lower investor risk, and boost the value of a company over its competitors.

Southwest Airlines is the only B2C example in this book, but its growth record is too good an example of sustainability and predictability to ignore. Southwest delivered 17 years (71 quarters) of profitable growth. It was the only U.S. airline to outperform the Dow Jones over that period. In fact, no other major airline was even profitable during that time. As you might expect, Southwest's stock increased 15-fold while the stock price of every other U.S. airline (Delta, American, US Airways, JetBlue, etc.) declined.

The B2B Road to SPPG

Sustainable, predictable, profitable growth is important to B2B and B2C alike. The destination for both types of companies is the same. Again, what varies between the two worlds are the keys parts of the journey which must be navigated in a very different manner.

As depicted in Exhibit 1-1, the staff functions of an organization, including Human Resources, Finance, Training, Manufacturing, and other back office Operations function very similarly in both B2B and B2C companies. In either type of organization you can utilize the same best practices and tactics. For example, B2B and B2C companies will manage Procurement in about the same fashion. As such, holding all other things constant, a tweak in any of these operational areas will not propel a B2B organization to SPPG, although a severe deficiency (such as rampant costs) could be keeping you from operating from a position of strength.

In any case, I do not focus on these areas since they are not the key differentiators for B2B business. Instead, *The B2B Executive Playbook* will focus on the areas that do affect how B2B companies reach SPPG: the "Go To Market" (GTM) areas of Strategy, Marketing, Service, Research and Development (R&D), and Sales. It is in these functions that the approach for B2B companies must be vastly different from B2C.

**Exhibit 1-1: Sustainable, Predictable, Profitable Growth—
A Different Go-To-Market Path for B2B Companies**

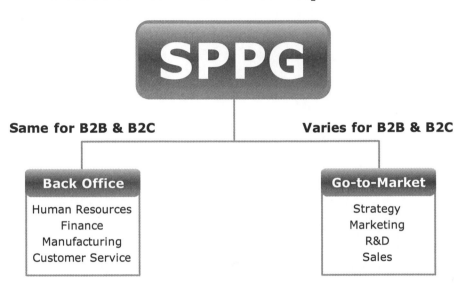

As I have discovered in working intimately with B2B companies and their executives, there is one concise path to get to SPPG:

- B2B companies must engage decision makers to help vet and formulate company strategy.

- B2B companies must become masters at leveraging the domain knowledge of their customer executive peers to discover game-changing innovation and deliver more value to the markets they serve.

- B2B companies must build and leverage customer executive relationships to accelerate profitable revenue growth.

The following chapters will explore why these elements must be central to every B2B company. I will first show you how the B2B world is a different game and why that will shape your game plan to sustainable, predictable, profitable growth.

CHAPTER 2

A DIFFERENT GAME

UNDERSTANDING HOW B2B IS UNIQUE

Michael Jordan is the greatest basketball player of all time. He could hit a game-winning basket under the most extreme pressure. He was so talented a player that he could carry a team to a championship. He did it in high school, college, the Olympics, and an astounding six times in the National Basketball Association (NBA). But when Jordan decided to play baseball, he couldn't hit a change up or a curve ball well enough to earn a spot on a minor league team. One person, two games, two very different outcomes: victorious domination and failure!

The parable of Michael Jordan's two careers is a story my colleagues and I see played out time and again in the B2B world. It comes to mind whenever we see a company struggling to meet expectations, despite being led by executives who have orchestrated meteoric climbs at other companies. We are reminded of Jordan when we meet with executives who cannot understand why initiatives and strategies they used successfully at other companies fail to deliver the goods in their new companies. And, we think again of Jordan, five-time NBA Most Valuable Player, when one of us needs to tell an executive he simply is playing a different game.

As in athletics, success for a leader in one kind of business does not automatically equate to success in another without a study of the game and some retooling of the playbook. The proper coaching can also be a big help. Unfortunately, B2B leaders often find it hard to obtain guidance on how to play their game. The most common sources of information—business books and conferences—typically showcase executives from high profile B2C companies. But B2B leaders can't simply adopt and apply lessons and approaches from B2C companies because it is a completely different experience for both the customer and the provider. Their needs are just different.

Living 50 miles up the road from consumer package goods (CPG) powerhouse Procter & Gamble and the thousands of employees who work there, the point of different games was driven home to me by a B2B CEO who once told me, "Never be the one who first hires someone out of P&G." Why wouldn't you? P&G produces professional managers who are smart, articulate, well-trained, and process-driven. They live and breathe the formula for success that has kept the company at the top of its game for decades. Why wouldn't any company welcome this experience and skill into their organization?

If you are a B2C company whose livelihood is built on a well-positioned brand and product that is preferred by a large share of the consumer market, you should be the first to snatch up an ex-P&G'er. He or she is a master of the B2C game and can bring P&G best practices to your organization. If you are a B2B company, however, that same job candidate may not be such a great hire. You should be looking for a professional who knows how to play the B2B game because the playbook for your success is very different. How often is that considered, though?

It's not. Think of how many times heralded executives from high profile B2C companies are snatched up to rescue floundering B2B companies. Because of their reputations and the caché of the companies they come from, these executives are almost always granted more authority (and budget) than normal. Emboldened by their previous B2C successes, these saviors almost invariably exercise their new clout promptly and with the utmost confidence by implementing the strategies that worked so well at their previous employer. Just as invariably, a train wreck ensues.

Does this mean that B2B companies should only hire B2B executives? Absolutely not. But whoever is hired must clearly understand the following three realities that distinguish the B2B world from the B2C world and use them to shape the company's playbook.

Reality #1: The Fate of a B2B Company Rests in the Hands of Relatively Few Customer Companies

When we first meet leaders at B2B companies, they tend to be very uncomfortable about sharing how many active customers they have. That's because there are thousands of B2B companies in which three or fewer customers account for 60 percent or more of total sales.

In many B2B companies, the loss of their biggest customer would put them out of business entirely. Many more could survive the loss, but would only recover after years of hard times. Think of the many automotive parts and services suppliers that sell to only one or two car makers. There used to be thousands of these companies who made a great living serving the Big Three automakers. But look at what happened to them with the consolidation and failure of the U.S. automotive industry. Today, in 10 minutes, I can drive by millions of square feet of vacant industrial space where the suppliers to General Motors, Ford, and Chrysler once had thriving businesses.

You could argue that the shakeout in the automotive industry is a lesson in the need for diversification along many lines. However, many of the suppliers who sought out foreign manufacturers are gone too. So are many suppliers who were experts in processes such as injection plastic molding that could be ported to other industries. Why? Their customer base was too small to handle the downside risk of losing even one big customer, and they never created a playbook that accommodated that reality.

A Tale of Two Companies

The significance of the much smaller customer base at B2B companies is best illustrated by a simple example that compares the number of customers and revenue at two leading companies.

Company A	Company B
$10 Billlion in Annual Revenue	$7 Billion in Annual Revenue
80 Million Customers Worldwide	100 Total Customers

Source: Geehan Group & Bernstein

A simple calculation tells the story. When you divide the revenues of each company by its customer base, you'll see that Company A receives $125 of revenue per customer, while Company B earns $70 million per customer. Clearly each and every customer at Company B has an immediate and direct impact on the health of the company. That fact alone should race the heartbeat of Company B executives.

But wait. Like every good tale, this one has a twist. Company B's customers are not created equal. In fact, there is a super-Pareto effect at work: In most cases the top 10 percent (just 10) of Company B customers generate more than 90 percent of total sales. On average, each of these 10 customers contributes $630 million (as opposed to straight-lined $70 million) to Company B's coffers. Revenue is not distributed equally per customer, so if one of these customers were to leave, the company would be drastically compromised. This is indeed a cautionary tale!

By the way, these are real companies. Company A is Starbucks, and Company B is Celestica, a Canadian supply chain services outsourcer. Exhibit 2-1 summarizes their respective revenue concentrations.

Exhibit 2-1: Revenue Concentration, Starbucks vs. Celestica

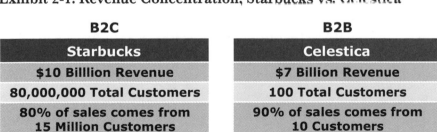

B2C	B2B
Starbucks	**Celestica**
$10 Billlion Revenue	$7 Billion Revenue
80,000,000 Total Customers	100 Total Customers
80% of sales comes from 15 Million Customers	90% of sales comes from 10 Customers

Source: Geehan Group & Bernstein

Starbucks and Celestica are not outliers. Exhibit 2-2 shows the revenue concentrations of a select group of other well-known B2C and B2B firms. In total, the B2C companies in this analysis derive $620 in revenue per customer, while the B2B companies derive almost $8.7 million in revenue per customer! It's also worth noting that the Pareto Principle holds true for the B2B companies listed: the top 20 percent of their customers generate more than 80 percent of their total sales.

Exhibit 2-2: Selected Revenue Concentrations, B2C vs. B2B

B2C			B2B		
Company	Customers	Revenue	Company	Customers	Revenue
Lowe's	14,000,000	$48 Billion	Oracle	4,000	$35 Billion
Walt Disney Company	100,000,000	$39 Billion	Accenture	471	$22 Billion
Apple Inc.	37,000,000	$76 Billion	GE Aviation	500	$17.6 Billion
Starbucks	70,000,000	$10.9 Billion	T-Systems	400	$13 Billion
Hallmark Cards	12,000,000	$4.4 Billion	Celestica	100	$7 Billion
Thor Industries	60,000	$2.4 Billion	Amdocs	198	$3.2 Billion
Facebook	750,000,000	$2 Billion	HCL	480	$3 Billion
Miami-Luken Inc.	550,000	$178 Million	Harris Broadcasting	2,000	$500 Million
Aurora Casket Co. Inc.	200,000	$163 Million	Woolpert	75	$200 Million
Lastar, Inc.	100,000	$120 Million	Interactive Intelligence Inc.	3,000	$166 Million
Klosterman Baking	4,000	$80 Million	Henny Penny	200	$127 Million
Dorothy Lane Market	60,000	$45 Million	Crown Partners	300	$20 Million
Average Revenue Per Customer:	$186		Average Revenue Per Customer:	$ 8,684,152	

Source: Bernstein and Geehan Group research

What does this concentration of revenue mean for a B2B company? Imagine Celestica losing two of its top 10 customers. Their loss of just these two top customers would result in a devastating 15 to 30 percent decline in annual revenue. Since many B2B companies have multi-year contracts with their customers, there would be a compounding effect year-over-year that would increase the decline. Conversely, Starbucks probably wouldn't know if it lost 1,000 of its top customers. In fact, no matter how many venti, nonfat, cinnamon-sprinkled, decaf lattes Starbucks' top 1,000 customers buy, if they all decided to switch to McDonald's McLattes, it wouldn't dent the company's revenues.

A few years ago when Tom Webster took over as CEO at Intesource, a B2B provider of spend management solutions based in Phoenix, Arizona, he discovered that 80 percent of the company's revenue came from just six customers. "The fact that only 6 customers controlled our fate was a major issue we needed to immediately address," Webster recalls. "Now we've got 12 customers who make up 80 percent of our revenue, which provides a much more sound and secure spread of revenue risk. But the reality of our business will always be that very few customers play a significant role in the health of our company." Even for $3.3 billion India-based HCL, more than 80 percent of their revenue comes from less than 100 accounts.

High revenue concentrations are a harsh reality in B2B, regardless of a company's size. Further, when the fate of a B2B lies in the hands of just a few customers, the power of these customers is enormous. "Once we realized that we only needed to secure a few dozen large customers in order to dominate our market, it changed the game for us," says Richard Hearn, the CEO of Crown Partners, a Midwestern provider of eBusiness solutions with $20 million in annual revenues. "Coming from a Procter & Gamble background, it was a complete mind-shift for me and other members of the leadership team."

What if your B2B company lost two of its top 10 accounts in the coming months? What would the impact be on the top line, bottom line, economies of scale, and the headcount and morale of your company? Would your company be able to recover from the loss, let alone fund growth and meet the expectations of its owners?

Reality #2: The Fate of a B2B Company Rests in the Hands of Just a Few People

If you are starting to feel a little claustrophobic, prepare to have your world shrink even further. In the B2B world purchasing decisions are made by just a few people. That's right, unlike in the B2C world, it's just a few people in a small number of customer companies that control a B2B company's destiny. Do you know who these people are in your customer companies? If so, how well is your company connected to them?

B2B Sales Involve Multiple Players

When I buy a song on iTunes, I play multiple roles:

- I'm the end user: I listen to songs I download to my iPod.

- I'm an influencer: I like the music of Dave Matthews and tell myself I'd enjoy hearing his band's latest release whenever I want.

- I'm my own purchasing agent: I decide that I'm willing to pay 99 cents for a new song, but not $1.49.

- And I'm the decision maker: I click the buy button.

Because I play all these roles as a consumer, it's not very hard for B2C companies to figure out how to market to me and others with a similar demographic, preference, buying habit, etc.

For B2B companies, on the other hand, these same four roles—end user, influencer, purchasing agent, and decision maker—are usually played by many different people. This creates complexity and confusion as companies try to focus their sales and marketing efforts. Exhibit 2-3 illustrates the number of people involved in an average purchase from four companies: Oracle; Crown Partners; restaurant equipment manufacturer Henny Penny; and information services provider Lexis-Nexis. For instance, the average customer for LexisNexis's legal research service is a mid-size law firm. Thus, there are 300 end users of the service, seven influencers (usually librarians and members of the technology or executive committee of the firm), one purchasing agent, and one decision maker (usually the firm's senior partner).

Exhibit 2-3: Four Roles, Multiple Players in Each Customer

	Oracle $40B	Henny Penny $127M	Crown Partners $20M	LexisNexis $2B
Decision Maker	1-2	1	1	1
Influencer	65	8	5	7
Purchasing	3	3	1	1
User	22,000	25,000	1,400	300

Source: Geehan Group

All these players are not equal in importance to a B2B seller, and, as I describe in the following pages, each provides a different level of input to the buying decision (see Exhibit 2-4).

Exhibit 2-4: Levels of Customer Input

Source: Geehan Group

The end users of your software, medical diagnostic equipment, or jet engines are important, of course, but they are not as important as conventional wisdom suggests. There may be thousands of them or more, but they can't renew the sales contract, upgrade to a more expensive solution, or decide to switch to a competitor. Neither can purchasing agents, unless you are selling a commodity, or you find yourself competing solely on price (and if that's the case, you probably need to add value to your offerings, and change your sales approach). Purchasing agents set standards and practices for purchasing and manage the procurement process, but they are not ultimately responsible for the decision to buy.

Influencers are involved in the buying decision by evaluating which solutions will best fulfill their companies' needs. Influencers also evaluate providers. They seek to discover if a B2B seller can do what it claims and whether it can work effectively with the customer company. Sometimes this process of evaluation and selection is straightforward. Typically, however, as the complexity of the solutions increases and they cut across organizational boundaries within the customer's company, so does the number of influencers involved in the sale. In fact, there may be dozens of these folks at any single customer firm and a B2B company needs to satisfy all of them.

Finally and ultimately, there are the decision makers. Usually residing near or at the top of the organizational hierarchy, these are the people who have the final vote; they decide to do the deal. They hear the recommendations of purchasing agents and influencers, and ask themselves questions designed to instill confidence in their final decisions, such as, "Will I enjoy working with this seller? Will it deliver what it is promising? Will it resolve any issues? Can I trust its people?"

At Celestica, there are less than 20 decision makers among the 10 customer companies that make up 90 percent of the company's annual revenues. Sometimes there is just one decision maker in a customer company, sometimes it is a two- or three-person executive committee that makes the final decision to buy. Regardless, in the B2B world, while a large number of people may be involved in a sale, very few of them control your fate.

To Whose Voice Do You Listen? Whose Voice Do You Hear?

Most B2B companies are already focused on engaging end users and influencers, and they can't avoid purchasing agents. But a surprisingly large number of them are either not paying enough attention to executive decision makers or are ignoring them altogether.

Like most B2B companies in the IT sector, Oracle is very focused on its end users. It's easy to see why Oracle would invest millions to connect to them. Events like Oracle OpenWorld, an annual conference that drew more than 40,000 people from the Oracle user community in 2010 and includes top entertainment (Sting and Tom Petty and the Heartbreakers are on the schedule for 2011), are critical to building and maintaining the loyalty of end users, and gaining insight into what they want and need in IT products and services.

But how does Oracle address the one or two executive customers in each of its major accounts who actually decide to buy its offerings? In 2004, Oracle's leaders asked themselves this question and quickly realized that most of their executive customers didn't have the time to attend multiday trade shows, no matter how interesting and enjoyable they were. So, Oracle's senior vice president and chief customer officer, Jeb Dasteel, was assigned the task of designing, launching, and overseeing an ongoing executive customer program. "End user relationships and input are critical to Oracle's success, but end users provide only one view of the market," explains Dasteel. "We realized how important additional input and relationships with other parts of the decision chain would be for our future. Without the perspective and insight of decision makers, we would be lacking a whole category of customer input today."

Oracle understands and taps into the power of executive customers, and that is a major reason why its performance has outpaced its competitors. Most B2B companies, however, are not as aware of executive customers as Oracle, and they devote their customer outreach efforts almost exclusively to the other levels of the customer hierarchy.

In fact, our research has found that the average B2B company spends 75 percent of its time and money marketing and selling to end users and purchasing agents, the two groups of customers who have the least say in purchase decisions. Influencers, who do play an important role in deciding purchases, receive substantially less attention. And decision makers, the executive customers who actually make the purchase, receive the least investment of all. This is far from optimal. (See Exhibit 2-5.)

Exhibit 2-5: Allocation of B2B Marketing and Sales Resources by Customer Level

Time/Money Allocation of Sales Resources

Customer Level	Typical	Optimal
Decision Maker Final authority/signature	10%	30%
Influencer Evaluation and due diligence of any potential purchase	15%	35%
User Those directly using the product or service	60%	30%
Purchasing Facilitate and govern buying protocols	15%	5%

Source: Geehan Group

When B2B companies do not actively and systemically engage their executive customers, there is a tremendous vacuum of critical information on both sides of the buying equation. On one, the B2B seller misses insight to the key business problems, challenges, aspirations, and priorities of their customer companies. The lack of this knowledge raises the risk of producing new products or services that will not succeed in the marketplace, as well as the loss of key accounts to competitive threats.

On the other side of the equation, if B2B companies do not engage their executive customers, how will these decision makers get the message about the business value the company provides? How will they learn about you as a business partner? How will they come to trust you? This level of understanding does not come through osmosis, nor is it communicated simply by delivering on your contracts. No, you have to do more.

But will they listen to you? Absolutely. There is a common misguided belief that executive customers are hard to reach and uninterested in talking to B2B solution sellers. We have always found, however, that executives are genuinely mystified by the lack of effort their key suppliers and other sellers make in reaching out to them. "When I became CEO, I was surprised I didn't get calls from most of our key suppliers," recalls Joe Morgan, CEO of $688 million Standard Register. This is even more surprising given the fact that Morgan was hired to grow the company after a period of restructuring. Therefore, understanding his expectations and aspirations for the company would have been critical to any B2B company that wanted to earn its business.

When companies neglect executive customers, the initial symptoms usually appear as sales woes. They include:

- Poor market reception of newly launched products and services or an unwillingness among customers to pay extra for new features and functionality

- Overwhelming price pressure and being treated like a commodity supplier

- The loss of key accounts or reductions in their volume

- Increased competition in profitable segments

- Sales engagements which are reactive and focused on today versus proactive and focused on the long-term

These are reliable indicators that the voice of the executive customer isn't being heard clearly. Often it means a company is listening only to the voice of end users and thus R&D, marketing, and sales are either not including or not fully communicating the business value essential to the executive decision maker.

Just as commonly, companies tend to listen to only the voice of their sales organization. Feedback from the sales team is very important, but it does have limitations. Most salespeople meet with users and purchasing agents, who tend to discuss lower-level issues, such as features and functionality. Salespeople are also very focused on overcoming objections and matching competitors' offerings. They extrapolate market needs from these interactions and bring that feedback to their employers as the voice of customer.

One major consequence of mistaking the voice of other players with the voice of the executive customer in B2B sales is very evident in studies of success rates of new products. IBM, AcuPoll, and other organizations have consistently found that newly launched products suffer from failure rates of 60-70 percent. Many of these failures result from neglecting executive customers. When the needs and concerns of executive customers are not built into market offerings, companies find themselves investing valuable resources in projects that add only incremental value or worse, actually diminish a company's ability to differentiate itself in the marketplace. This is why it's so important that innovation is relevant …meaning that there is at least one point of differentiation in new offerings for which decision makers are willing to pay.

Reality #3: B2B Companies Rely Upon the Knowledge and Acumen of Customers

Consumers can provide input and feedback on a product, but it is usually limited to what they like and don't like and, perhaps, what else they might want. But in the B2C world, customers can't typically tell a company how to design a better product or help engineer it. They don't have that kind of expertise.

In fact, consumers are rarely experts regarding the products and services they buy. In a blind taste test, for example, 90 percent of consumers couldn't tell a $10 bottle of wine from a $100 bottle. Nor could they tell the difference between tap water and a $5 bottle of Fiji water. That's why sophisticated and highly emotional marketing and branding programs can yield premium results in the B2C world—they are the main basis for product differentiation among consumers.

By contrast, B2B decision makers have knowledge extremely valuable to the companies selling to them. Consider GE Aviation, the world's leading provider of jet engines. Its customers, which include major airlines and the military, can provide expert guidance on all aspects of the jet engines they buy. They know how the design of an engine impacts thrust, range, payload, maintenance needs, FAA compliance, financial cost/payback, and so on. In the B2B world, your customers may not be familiar with your offerings per se, but they usually know their industries better than those who supply it, and they know how to evaluate your solutions in light of their needs. They aren't going to be swayed by marketing collateral; they will scrutinize, compare, benchmark, and test your offerings. And they will also seek out expert advice from peers and third parties for references and validation.

This goes double or triple for executive customers. Think about the domain knowledge of a CIO who has worked in the financial services sector his entire career. He is an expert in IT and his industry. He has networked and attended countless trade shows and educational events. The CIO has an unparalleled ability to cut through the sales jargon and understand the true value of solutions offered to his company. In most situations, the CIO also knows more about how to effectively deploy technology within his firm and industry than virtually all the companies seeking to sell him products and services. And when he doesn't know something, he can simply phone a trusted peer.

To successfully serve this executive customer, a B2B company must understand his needs, priorities, requirements, and operating environment almost as well as he does. There is too much at risk in his world—asset security, the customer's experience, privacy, government compliance, and the CIO's reputation and career—for him to work with a company that doesn't understand. The same holds true in every B2B industry, whether it's oil and gas, high pressure valves, medical equipment, scientific journals, procurement services, jet engine manufacturing, media distribution services, business process outsourcing, etc.

The Impact of the B2B Realities on Margin

The reputation of a company and its brands are primary determinants of its margins. Reputation is how a company is viewed in the marketplace—what it is known for, how its culture is viewed, and, most importantly, what the market believes about the value of its offerings. These are all external perceptions, but in both B2C and B2B, they add up to a sort of capital that accrues as customers willingly pay a premium price for a company's offerings. Only then will margins expand predictably over a sustained period of time.

What differs in B2C and B2B companies is how corporate and brand reputation is created. In the B2C world, reputation is defined by elements such as advertising, package design, and the experience of using the product. B2C companies invest millions to understand the demographic and geographical nuances of customers in order to position and manage their corporate and brand reputations in the mass markets of the consumer sector. Retailers, such as Starbucks and Target, add the look of the store and the behavior of employees to the mix.

In the B2B world, corporate and brand reputation is composed of the same elements, but in very different configurations. The priority and weighting of the elements are altered by the three realities discussed above.

As we've seen, the people you are selling to within your customer companies are usually industry veterans with high levels of domain expertise. Simply put, they're living what you're selling. These customers aren't going to pay a premium for your offerings because you've got a cool logo, a catchy tagline, or a slick PowerPoint presentation. What do they respond to? Business value. And how do they determine that value exists in an offering? In addition to their own knowledge, they rely on their peers. For example, surveys of CIOs consistently find they rate peer input as the most credible and trusted source of information about products and services.

Thus, the path to a premium reputation in the B2B realm is through your current customers. It is how they perceive and describe your offerings and what they think and say about working with your company and your ability to deliver what you promise that ultimately determines your company's reputation. And the higher these customers are on the corporate ladder, the greater the impact of their opinions and recommendations. That's why companies that successfully attain sustainable, predictable, profitable growth, such as Oracle, seek to anchor their reputations as high as possible within their customers' organizations. The good will of end users is important, but the good will of the person who makes the decision to buy is far more important to B2B companies that are trying to maximize their margins.

"Customers are your brand managers," explains Tom Webster, who was a senior marketing executive at several B2B companies prior to becoming CEO at Intesource. "They establish your brand and significantly impact its perception. If you earn their support, your customers can accelerate brand growth more effectively than anything else. Nothing boosts our position like a CFO [Intesource's primary executive customer] sharing and endorsing the benefits of our solutions or working with us. The impact of his words is unmatched, and you can measure the return financially. His peers will assume that the value and pricing has been vetted and accepted, so they have little to question when negotiating with you. Margins soar!"

Moving up the B2B Relationship Continuum

A little more than a decade ago, India-based IT services outsourcer HCL Technologies successfully broke into the U.S. market with a "low cost" value proposition, like many other Indian service providers. But after a few years that proposition became less compelling, mainly because prices equalized as competition heated up. Many U.S.-based competitors, including IBM, Hewlett-Packard, and Accenture, lowered their cost bases (often by setting up operations in India) in order to replicate the cost structure of off-shore labor providers and remove the significant price decrease as a point of differentiation.

In response, HCL beefed up its capabilities in order to provide more value to its customers. The company transformed its value proposition moving beyond commodity-like outsourcing services to acting as a problem solver and often co-engineering applications and products with its customers. But HCL has encountered a dilemma that commonly arises when a company seeks to change its positioning in the market: although its existing customers have come to understand, appreciate, and pay for the added value HCL is offering, its target market (Fortune 2000) still perceives the company as simply a low-cost labor provider.

The "perception gap" that HCL is battling has a financial impact on its revenue growth and margins. As HCL's global CMO Krishnan Chatterjee explains, this is where and why reputation and market positioning matters. "We have the proof points which can support our desired position as problem solver and trusted advisors. My responsibility now is to close the gap between the perception in the marketplace and the reality that we are capable of delivering to IT leaders around the globe."

The following graph (Exhibit 2-6) depicts how branding and margin collide and impact one another in B2B companies. As the B2B company improves its position with decision makers, the higher premium these decision makers are willing to pay for perceived value. If you are stuck in the position of "commodity supplier" (whether or not that is the position you think you hold), you will only be able to command commodity pricing and the low margins that come along with it. To increase the value of your brand, you must move the market's (more precisely, collective decision makers') perception of you towards Problem Solver and Trusted Advisor in order to secure consistently higher margins needed for profitable growth. As I show in the graph, failing to improve your position, or the market's perception of you, leaves a tremendous loss in margin.

Exhibit 2-6: The B2B Relationship Continuum—How Brand Perception Gaps Affect Margins in the B2B Sector

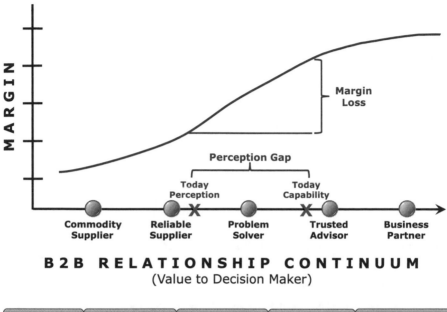

Commodity Supplier	Reliable Supplier	Problem Solver	Trusted Advisor	Business Partner
• Price • Procurement • Raw materials • Do-it-yourself	• One of many that you can count on • Dependable • Consistent • Process oriented	• Addresses defined issues • Specialized and limited in scope and perspective • Innovator	• Called in to help think through, identify issues, opportunities • Design overarching plans	• Shared cost and financial outcome • Long-term commitment • Interdependent

Source: Geehan Group

As a B2B company raises its reputation among executive customers and moves to the right of the Continuum, the premium decision makers are willing to pay for solutions begins to rise in their minds. If the B2B seller is stuck on the left side of the Relationship Continuum (again, in the minds of executive customers, whether or not that perception is an accurate reflection of reality), the company will only be able to command commodity pricing and the low margins that go with it.

B2B companies such as HCL need a marketing strategy and supporting tactics which are capable of positioning them farther to the right on the Relationship Continuum. Executive customers are indispensible for such a move. They are the opinion makers who matter the most and they drive the perception of a company in the B2B marketplace. Tactically speaking, they are also the peers their colleagues look to for information and recommendations. Credible third parties, such as industry analysts from research services like Forrester and Gartner, and messaging campaigns that repeat and amplify the perceptions of executive customers are useful and effective supporting tactics too, but executive customers are the cornerstone of reputation-building initiatives.

Decision makers become even more important as a company moves farther to the right on the Relationship Continuum. As B2B companies seek to assume roles as trusted advisors and business partners, they need enthusiastic executive customers who are willing to share their stories with their peers. It is very difficult to make a case that a B2B company is capable of acting as a trusted advisor or a valued business partner if no customer will step up to confirm or validate its claims.

The B2B Path to SPPG

In this chapter, I have discussed the critical differences between B2B and B2C companies which can be boiled down to three main points:

- Revenue is controlled by relatively few customers

- Decision makers are not users

- B2B executives must leverage the domain knowledge of their customer executive decision maker peers

The needs, hopes, and aspirations of decision makers must be intimately understood and addressed because they literally hold the fate of your company in their decision-making hands. You can gain this critical knowledge by actively engaging decision makers to drive your company to SPPG. The balance of the *Playbook* will show you how they will help develop your strategy, fuel innovation, design marketing and sales plans, and align your leadership team.

CHAPTER 3

SIX BENEFITS, FOUR STEPS

TAPPING THE POWER OF EXECUTIVE CUSTOMERS

*V*ery few B2B companies have fully engaged and developed substantive relationships with their executive customers. Most companies ignore executive customers, often not realizing how important they are to B2B success. Instead, they focus their relationship-building efforts on lower levels of the customer hierarchy. Other B2B companies relegate relationships with executive customers to their sales and marketing departments. Unfortunately, however, this usually results in an approach to executive customer relationship-building that treats these most important decision makers as sales targets. All of these companies are missing valuable opportunities to drive SPPG.

Companies that adopt a more strategic mindset in their approach to executive customers and in the development of these invaluable relationships can capture six opportunities:

- Market and leadership team alignment

- Strategic insight

- Marketing direction

- Improved sales retention, penetration, and references

- Innovation that is relevant and important to decision makers and a critical mass of the market

- Sustainable, predictable, profitable growth (SPPG)

Market and Leadership Team Alignment

The leadership teams of many B2B companies are beset with conflict. Often, this conflict is based on competing opinions about how to best move the company ahead. Some members of the team have rogue ideas; others categorically resist change; still others have a "not-invented-here" mindset that can blind them to external developments that could have a powerful effect on the company and its markets. Further, the personal ambitions of leadership team members can stifle alignment and consensus, and limit support for critical initiatives.

There is no better means of overcoming these sources of conflict than executive customers. When the leadership team of a B2B company works directly with executive customers, it becomes more unified and aligned. These customers, especially when gathered together in a group, provide an unimpeachable source of information, insight, and opinion that acts as a filter—quickly dispatching the conflicting views that can splinter a company's strategic focus or create barriers to change. An executive customer collective provides a single point of reference for the entire leadership team—in contrast to the information overload and endless debates, which can paralyze companies when key decisions and faster and bolder moves are most needed.

We've seen first-hand how executive customers deliver this benefit at many of our client companies. At Springer Science+Business Media, a global leader in scientific and professional publishing, customer executives have provided valuable input that enabled the company's leaders and directors to make important decisions about pricing and business models in an industry that has been buffeted by technological change. Executive customers also provide Springer's leaders with the clarity and focus they needed to speed market and product planning, and build internal support and performance.

Executive customers have had a similar effect at Wells Fargo, which has quadrupled the number of its programs aimed at engaging top customer decision makers from 5 to 12 in recent years. "Our executive customer programs have been incredible for our leadership team," explains senior vice president Jeff Tinker. "They continue to validate our challenges, our thinking, and where we should be going.

They definitely help keep us aligned to their needs, which in turn ensures greater internal alignment."

Strategic Insight

Because executive customers are the leaders of their companies, they face many of the same business challenges with which B2B executives grapple. Both must make the same hard decisions involving investment trade-offs, prioritization, budgeting strains, and resource limitations— and they must make them in good time and deliver returns that justify their decisions. Executive customers not only relate to the challenges B2B sellers face, they also have the expertise in the industry to offer tangible strategic insight on how to address them.

When this insight, experience, and knowledge is combined with the internal expertise of a B2B leadership team, it creates a springboard for solving what often seem to be intractable management problems. And of course, the market insights of executive customers, individuals who have the most B2B buying clout, are unparalleled. They bring new perspectives and fresh ideas that give B2B leadership teams the clarity and confidence they need to make bold strategic decisions.

As Lisa Campbell, the general manager at Autodesk's geospatial business unit attests, "Our customer executive programs have been instrumental in both our business and product planning. They have impacted so many areas of our business and have definitely changed our approach and our results in positive ways."

Marketing Direction

Since executive customers are leading the industries to which B2B companies are selling, their perspective and input can have an outsized effect on marketing effectiveness. They can be tapped to better understand the market perceptions of a B2B company, its value proposition, and its messaging. They can tell a leadership team how their branding efforts might be off target. Executive customers can offer information regarding what, where, and how to market offerings to maximize a B2B company's return on investment (ROI).

Sometimes the value of this feedback is instantly apparent. For example, Intesource recently previewed an upcoming marketing campaign for a group of its executive customers. They said it wouldn't work and told the company why in some detail. "Being a former CMO, it was a tough pill to swallow," recalls CEO Webster. "So I tested it in a small way. Our executive customers were right. We would have blown more than 20 percent of our total annual marketing budget on the initial campaign, but we adjusted it as they recommended, and the revised campaign yielded huge dividends."

HCL Technologies received insight from executive customers to develop a global branding program. "Our executive customers provide a mechanism for us to view ourselves through our customers' eyes," says CMO Chatterjee. "With this vision, we were able to design much more credible messages that far exceeded our expectations."

Sales Retention, Penetration, and References

Bonds are formed whenever people come together for a common purpose, and programs designed to engage executive customers are no exception. In fact, these B2B programs are the best and most consistent way to develop strong bonds with key accounts. They lead to increases in account retention and penetration, and they create a pool of references that is a powerful tool for winning new accounts.

The sales benefits are by-products of well-developed executive customer relationships. When a B2B company fully engages an executive customer, the customer becomes invested in the seller's future; he or she begins to care about the seller and wants to see it do well in the marketplace. It is analogous to a new recruit in the military. As boot camp progresses, the recruit begins to internalize a larger mission—to protect his or her country and the members of the unit. Often this bond becomes so strong that a lifelong connection is formed. The same basic dynamic comes into play in executive customers programs. It is just human nature.

Executive customers can become passionate advocates of B2B sellers, both within their home organizations and the markets at large. "Even in the accounts where we aren't performing great," says Oracle's Dasteel, "when executive customers participate in our engagement programs, they continue to buy, buy more, and even help us convert prospects to customers."

This isn't just talk. As you might expect, a high-tech company like Oracle has quantified the returns of their executive customer programs. A review of their top 400 accounts showed significant differences between customers involved in relationship programs and those who are not (see Exhibit 3-1). Oracle hasn't shared the numbers, but we know that each percentage point of improvement equates to increases in revenue growth and profitability. And much of this growth is in existing accounts, where margins are almost always higher because they incur lower sales and on-boarding costs.

Exhibit 3-1: Oracle's Return on Executive Customer Programs

Oracle Customers Engaged in Customer Programs vs. Those Not Engaged	
Overall Satisfaction Rating	24% Greater When Engaged in a Customer Program
Willing to Recommend	19% Greater When Engaged in a Customer Program
Continue Purchasing	25% Greater When Engaged in a Customer Program

Source: Oracle Corporation

Our own research, conducted in more than 70 client companies, reveals substantially higher percentages across industries. For instance, we found the percentage of decision-maker customers "willing to recommend" increased by more than 270 percent when they participate in an executive engagement program (see Exhibit 3-2).

Exhibit 3-2: Results of Executive Customer Programs: Geehan Group Clients

Customers Who Participate in Executive Customer Programs	
Retention	+30%
Account Growth	+300%
Executives Willing to Recommend	+270%
Overall Satisfaction	+30%

Source: Geehan Group

Anecdotal evidence also supports these figures:

- At Intesource, the growth in accounts that participated in executive customer programs rose 100 percent in a two-year period. Referrals also rose: one customer referred and helped secure three new customers in a six-month timeframe, a substantial number in a company that had 30 customers.

- At HCL Technologies, executive customer programs contributed to a customer retention rate above 94 percent. More than 70 percent of sales growth over a four-year period came from existing customers who were involved in these programs. Since the launch of HCL's Executive Customer Council, they have not lost one of their participating customers.

Relevant Innovation

The ability to produce innovative products and services is a much-vaunted corporate quality, but innovation initiatives also consume a huge amount of corporate resources, often with little or no return. Consider Xerox's famed Palo Alto Research Center (PARC), which pioneered many innovations, including the mouse and the graphical user interface that produces the windows and icons you see on your computer monitor. Xerox funded these innovations, but never successfully commercialized them. The lesson of PARC for B2B companies is that the only product and service innovation worth pursuing is innovation that is both relevant to your customers and for which they will pay a premium.

Relevant innovation also goes beyond run-of-the-mill improvements to the features and functions of existing products. Most "next generation" products companies bring to market aren't game-changing enablers of business transformation. Think of the many versions of Windows that Microsoft has released over the years. How many represented relevant innovation and how many found a market simply because they were preloaded on new PCs?

Historically, B2B companies have struggled to produce relevant innovation. Research shows that new product success rates are only in the 30-40 percent range. One reason for this poor performance is that B2B companies have followed the B2C mindset in developing new products—they focus on the needs and desires of end users. The problem, of course, is that end users are not usually the decision makers in the B2B world. Further, although the B2C approach can work for product improvements and updates, end users rarely provide the level of feedback needed for B2B companies to produce new offerings containing the degree of business innovation and transformation that motivates executive decision makers to buy.

At Wells Fargo, executive customers helped transform the bank's innovation focus. Executive customers came up with the idea of a mobile portal so that CFOs could easily access important information about their accounts when they were away from their computers. The Wells Fargo executive customer collective, a group of 15 financial leaders drawn from the bank's most important commercial accounts, assisted throughout the development process—helping define the main components of the portal, performing reviews, serving as beta testers, and providing input and feedback on the go-to-market strategy.

When executive customers are involved in the entire innovation process, the chances of producing a hit are significantly increased. Similarly, they can identify a potential flop early in the process. Due to the success of financial programs and services in the consumer and small business markets, such as Intuit's Quicken and QuickBooks, Wells Fargo considered offering commercial accounting services and delivering them online via their portal. It seemed a natural extension, but when the company vetted the idea with its executive customers, the response was overwhelmingly negative. They said they would not buy accounting services from the bank; what they really wanted was an easier way to integrate their existing accounting packages with their accounts. Their feedback saved Wells Fargo time, money, and credibility in the marketplace.

Relevant innovation extends to mergers and acquisitions (M&A) too, because often B2B companies buy innovation. Therefore, executive customers can play a valuable role in the M&A process as well. Oracle, for example, has acquired more than 60 companies to build out their offerings since 2005. Executive customers helped the company identify solution gaps and even suggested acquisition targets that weren't on its radar. "Whether we develop it or acquire innovation, it must be relevant to the customer's world," says Jeb Dasteel. "Our executive customers make sure we invest properly."

HCL Technologies has tapped executive customers to drive its efforts to create an innovative new business model. "Our executive customers have not only helped us create innovative products and services, but even more importantly, they have driven the transformation of our business model," says Anubhav Saxena, global vice president of marketing and strategy of HCL's ISD unit. "With so many directions and paths we could pursue, the clarity and direction our executive customers have provided is unmatched. Redefinition of our value proposition on Business Aligned IT, conceptualization and eventual co-development of HCL's Gold Standard, and the reinforcement of our onshore/right-shore Global Delivery Model investments including brand enhancing recommendations are some examples."

The End Result: SPPG

The first five benefits of engaging executive customers—market and leadership team alignment, strategic insight, marketing direction, increased sales, and relevant innovation—produce sustainable, predictable, profitable growth. By listening to these decision makers and investing resources in areas that are viable and important to them, you can avoid wasting time, energy, and money in areas where there is little or no business value, and capture the sixth and final benefit of *The B2B Executive Playbook*: SPPG.

The value of executive customers—one of the most underdeveloped resources in the B2B sector—is difficult to overstate. But since the most credible advice and recommendations come from peers, don't take my word for it. Listen to Intesource's CEO Tom Webster: "We opened the company kimono to our executive customers…the good, the bad, and the ugly. That was very hard, but the relationships and the trust that were established as a result are beyond description. Our executive customers not only assisted in the design of our next generation of solutions, marketing plans, sales training, customer support programs, and pricing models, they also helped design our future."

The facts support Webster's claim: within two years of launching their executive customer initiative, Intesource, which had been on the brink of closing its doors, was recording revenue growth and margins that were well above industry averages.

The B2B Executive Playbook

So, we've studied the B2B game and now know why and how well-developed relationships with executive customers drive SPPG. What's next? We need a proven strategy and an approach for tapping into this powerful source of insight and growth—a playbook for B2B executives.

The B2B Executive Playbook has been developed with more than 20 years experience assisting B2B companies as they adopt, implement, and manage executive customer programs. We've seen it work time and again for the companies featured in these pages, including Oracle, HCL, Intesource, Springer Science+Business Media, Intel, Autodesk, Harris Broadcast, Crown Partners, and Wells Fargo, as well as many others. This playbook is composed of a four-step process for developing executive customer relationships in a way that ensures a company can capture all six benefits.

The four steps are not a typical process that must be executed in its entirety to produce some kind of output. Instead, they are a programmatic approach that has both an incremental and a cumulative effect on corporate performance. As B2B companies successfully implement the first step in the process, their revenue begins to grow and their profitability increases. With each new step, these metrics improve—profitable growth becomes sustainable and predictable (see Exhibit 3-3).

Exhibit 3-3: The Cumulative Effect of *The B2B Executive Playbook*

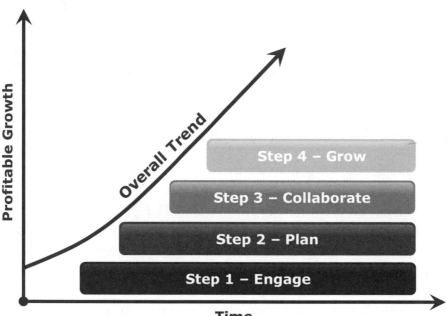

Source: Geehan Group

Step 1: Engage

When B2B leaders have a major decision to make, especially regarding risk-laden issues such as fundamental changes in business models, core capabilities, or product/service portfolios, they typically bring together internal players who can provide insight and perspective. But how often do these same leaders include their company's executive customers in their deliberations? These are the customers who hold the fate of the company in their hands, and they drive the markets on which B2B companies depend. These are the customers who vote with their dollars about the viability and relevance of innovation, and the B2B companies with whom they will do business. When you think of executive customers in these terms, the only real surprise is that any B2B leader would leave them out of important decisions.

That is why the first step in *The B2B Executive Playbook* is to engage executive customers and connect them to the leadership team of your company. The most effective way to accomplish this is to create a market collective that

> **Market Collective**
>
> **A group of decision makers or executive customers drawn from a B2B company's key accounts in terms of strategic importance and revenue contribution.**

is composed of the key decision makers in the most important companies in your customer base. Because this market collective is a vital source of alignment and information for the leadership team of any B2B company, this is the foundational element of *The B2B Executive Playbook*—it is the element that provides the engine and initial trajectory of SPPG.

When done correctly, the creation of a market collective, and its systematic connection to the leadership team of your company, becomes the basis on which decisions are made regarding strategy, business model innovation, planning, marketing, innovation and development, acquisitions, and sales and service. This step in the *Playbook* addresses a multitude of common problems that plague decision making within B2B companies, including:

- An overly intense focus on internal considerations or end users

- Reactive versus proactive strategic thinking

- Risk aversion and resistance to change

- A poor grasp of the marketplace and other externalities, including globalization, niche competition, and technological change

- Internal conflict and lack of support within the leadership team

The Engage step is the first step in the process of addressing and fixing these and many related issues. This step is discussed in detail in Chapter 4.

Step 2: Plan

Strategy guru Michael Porter describes strategy as simply "what your firm will and will not do." That sounds straightforward, but B2B leadership teams that unanimously agree on what their companies should and shouldn't do are not easy to find. Much more commonly, the strategic planning process in B2B companies is overly complex and too far removed from the marketplace. And in the end, it produces a plan in which the company's leaders have little or no confidence. Too often, the strategic part of the process gets shortchanged for the planning part. Strategy meetings become sales planning and budgeting sessions, or they get hung up on short-term decision-making, none of which provide long-term direction, much less a plan for sustainable, predictable, profitable growth. It's no wonder that leadership surveys conducted by McKinsey & Co. have consistently found that 70 percent of global executives are dissatisfied with their strategic planning process.

If they hope to attain sustainable, predictable, profitable growth, B2B companies require strategic plans that account for the nature of revenue concentration, the differentiation of users from decision makers, and the overall complexity of the B2B buying process. Executive customers can provide this focus and build confidence in the strategic planning process and the plan it produces. In Chapter 5, we'll discuss how B2B companies can utilize their executive customers to drive a market-aligned strategic planning process.

Step 3: Collaborate

Most R&D efforts in B2B companies engage with end users instead of decision makers. As a result, most innovation is merely incremental feature-function enhancement that fails to wow the market. Executive customers help solve this problem in the third step of the *Playbook*. They provide an expanded level of exposure to the marketplace that better aligns development teams and often uncovers new opportunities for transformational offerings. This is account-based innovation.

Executive customers raise the attention level of development teams above the end users, enabling them to rise above feature and functionality improvements. At Harris Corporation's Broadcast Communications division, for example, direct engagement

Account-Based Innovation

A platform for a B2B company to work one-on-one with an executive customer company to collaborate and co-develop custom solutions for mutual advantage.

with executive customers keeps the development team not only aware of specific account needs, but plugged into future opportunities. "Without that, the development team would be guessing or simply reacting to the market, and that's a recipe for failure," says division president Harris Morris. "Instead, the relationships we have built with our strategic accounts enable us to help design the industry's future standard, not follow the standard…a much preferred position."

Keeping R&D close to the market at the decision-maker level significantly increases the ROI that B2B companies achieve on their innovation initiatives. By developing solutions that are aligned with and embraced by customers, companies can boost their position in the marketplace while reducing the threat of commoditization. The primary benefits of account-driven innovation include:

- Customers surface opportunities your company would have otherwise missed

- Customers participate in R&D programs and provide testimonials

- Customer-retention rates rise and sole-sourced sales opportunities increase

- Visibility, credibility, and access within customer organizations are improved

- Customer satisfaction levels rise

- Collaborative innovation yields a competitive advantage and a market-entry barrier that new and niche competitors can't overcome

Step 3 of *The B2B Executive Playbook* is discussed in greater detail in Chapter 6.

Step 4: Grow

In step 4 of *The B2B Executive Playbook*, marketing and sales take center stage. The goal of this step is to deliver profitable sales growth in a predictable and sustainable fashion. This is achieved by transforming executive customers into advocates who willingly proselytize on behalf of your company. Such an advocate is a far more effective sale-closer than any other tactic or technique.

Advocacy is the highest level of participation, but it is not something you can demand of executive customers. Rather, it must be cultivated. This cultivation process takes place throughout the first three steps in the *Playbook*, which brings the decision makers in key customer accounts closer to your business, and paves the way for the development of loyal advocates who will voluntarily work on your behalf. Without this requisite pre-work, the loyalty and advocacy of executive customers will not exist.

Once executive customers become advocates, they will become your most powerful marketing and sales assets. They are indispensible as B2B companies seek to expand their portfolios, enter new markets, position their company farther along the value continuum and drive SPPG.

> ### Executive Customer Advocates + Prospects = Explosive Sales Growth.

Executive customer advocates are potent weapons for acquiring new business. Marketing, for instance, can utilize these valuable assets by holding peer forums, such as industry networking and educational events, in order to put these advocates in the same room with prospective customers. "Our executive customers and decision makers at other companies in their industries enjoy getting together to share ideas and discuss issues that are central to their success," explains Keith Hawk, senior vice president of sales at LexisNexis. "It is important for them to feel safe, in a collaborative environment where they have time to think…and are not being sold to. These discussions provide prospective customers with the clarity and confidence needed to make key decisions. For us, the result is more new customers and a big sales boost." Take special note of Hawk's point about not selling: executive customers will do all the selling you need as they share their stories through formal means such as presentations, case studies, and panel discussions, as well as informal means such as meals, industry forums, and entertainment events.

This final step of the *Playbook* is discussed in more depth in Chapter 7.

B2B Executive Playbook Scorecard

Results. This is the bottom line all business leaders seek help to achieve. My colleagues and I have worked in the B2B space for so many years that we know how important it is to be able to show results for any investment. In fact, we scratch our heads each time we see programs and initiatives approved and executed repeatedly without any measured results. We know that programs are often funded for various reasons, including "we have always done it," or "we will miss the boat if we don't," or "our competitor is doing it." But, wouldn't it be better if you had an actual yardstick and some measurements to boost your confidence before opening the purchase order?

Exhibit 3-4 presents the scorecard we use to measure results from *Playbook* activities. This scorecard shows just some of the quantifiable results we have seen B2B companies achieve when they engage, collaborate, and leverage the advocacy of customer decision makers. Benchmarking these areas both before and after the implementation of *Playbook* activities serves as a powerful, objective justification to fund the necessary programs, as well as a testimonial your B2B company is heading in the right direction.

Exhibit 3-4: *The B2B Executive Playbook* Scorecard

Area	Typical Results
Organization	
Strategy	• Ability to generate sustainable, predictable, profitable growth
Market Alignment	• Increased clarity and confidence on market needs and aspirations
Internal Alignment	• Depoliticize/breakdown barriers of risk aversion; confidence to get organizational buy-in to make bolder and transformational decisions
Marketing	
Marketing Positioning	• Rebalancing of marketing budgets to maximize overall ROI • More effective decision maker programs • Greater ability to prove program ROI • Clarity on rebalancing marketing dollars
Offerings	
Success Rate of New Product Introductions	• 27% increase in new offering success
Number of New Products in Development (Innovation)	• Increase in transformational vs. incremental offerings
Cost Avoidance (Invalidated/ Off-the-Mark Product Releases)	• 36% reduction in development of failed offerings
Acquisitions	• Acquire and integrate more relative and high-value offerings
Customer Service	
Satisfaction Levels	• 15% increase in satisfaction
Cross-sell/Add-on Sales Opportunities	• 12% revenue increase from additional opportunities
Sales	
Reference Accounts (Decision-Maker Levels)	• 300% increase • Ability to have much more robust complete reference program
Customer Retention	• 22% increase in retention
"Wallet Share" Spending from Current Customers	• 12% increase in Council Member purchases
New Customers	• 12% increase in new sales

Just Four Steps

In today's complex B2B world, it may seem like four steps to SPPG are overly simplistic. But consider what else can be accomplished in just four steps. In the world of music, there is a four-chord progression (G, D, E^M, C) that has generated thousands of hits and driven the careers of some of the most successful artists in history, including rock musicians Bob Dylan, Michael Jackson, The Who, Elton John, Journey, Alicia Keyes, Jimmy Buffet, and Jack Johnson. Songs like The Beatles' "Let it Be," U2's "With or Without You," Jason Mraz's "I'm Yours," and many others follow this same progression. These chords provide a playbook for writing a great song. Just four chords.

Likewise, *The B2B Executive Playbook* has just four steps: Engage, Plan, Collaborate, and Grow. By properly implementing and sequencing them, you can drive both SPPG and your career. In the B2B world to date there has been no parallel.

CHAPTER 4

ENGAGE

CREATING A MARKET COLLECTIVE

Established in 1842, German- and Dutch-based Springer Science+Business Media is the world's largest publisher of science, technology, and medical (STM) books, and the second-largest publisher of STM journals. In the mid-1990s, Springer, like all publishers, was selling journals through subscription agents, and books through trade and specialty booksellers. Publishing was a staid, static industry at that time; in fact, content distribution hadn't changed very much since Gutenberg invented the printing press. "There was no need for interaction," recalls Syed Hasan, Springer's president and global sales leader. "We had one person who talked to the libraries to get a feel for their needs—to take the temperature of things. Other than that, there was limited interaction with customers. We left that up to third-party agents."

Then came the Internet and in 1996, Adobe's introduction of the PDF format. The Internet created an entirely new distribution model for publishing. PDFs provided a universally readable digital format that offered publishers a way to protect their content from piracy and mass reproduction. Similar to the impact that Apple's iTunes had on the music industry, the Internet and the PDF led to radical shifts in the publishing value chain.

Springer realized that these shifts required its old methods of connecting with customers be updated. But what to do? Should the publisher try to go directly to end users—the millions of readers of its materials? Should it boost its sales force and begin selling more aggressively to librarians and other large customers? Or, should it maintain its distribution network of subscription agents and booksellers?

When faced with such questions some leadership teams would seek out internal opinions and feedback. Others might make a command decision on their own. But Springer did something smarter. It engaged its key executive customers—in this case, the leaders of consortia groups and head librarians in the company's best and most valuable accounts. "We asked them what they would be interested in," says Hasan. "As a result, we were able to move forward at a critical juncture, not just within our company but within the market at large."

We've already seen why executive customers are critical to B2B success. Now we will explore how companies can attract their attention, most effectively engage them, and create sustainable interactions that lead to mutually beneficial relationships.

Defining "Engagement"

Like "innovation," the word "engage" is overused in the business world, and means different things in different companies. When I talk about engagement, I mean the ability of a B2B company to bring the decision makers within their top accounts into their organizations in an ongoing, collaborative, and advisory fashion. Engagement means executive customers are talking to your leadership team directly and without filters. They are thinking about and describing how your company can add value to their businesses. They are actively involved in the development of your products and services, and your strategic, marketing, and sales planning processes. Engagement means that executive customers are invested in your success. In short, they are an extension of your team.

Given all the demands and pressures on executive customers, it may seem idealistic and unrealistic to expect them to make this kind of commitment to a B2B company. But there are B2B companies that are highly successful at consistently and systematically bringing these decision makers together into marketing collectives and engaging with them. And they are outperforming their competitors as a result.

To facilitate engagement, Oracle connects executive customers from their most important accounts directly with its leadership team, including company co-founder, chairman, and CEO Larry Ellison, and the members of the board of directors. Crown Partners has also created a market collective and connected it directly to its leadership team. The collective helps Crown's leaders align with market needs, create clear priorities, and generate greater growth and predictability for both top and bottom lines.

"When the entire Crown Partners leadership team participates, it reduces wasted time," adds CEO Richard Hearn. Hearn found that market collectives shortcut the process of getting functional heads on board when major new initiatives are proposed and launched. "There is much less bickering, and fewer power-plays and budgeting debates. The executive customers in the market collective provide an external reference point that neutralizes unhealthy and unproductive behaviors." And as Hearn notes, "The market is the driver, not any one group or person within our company."

Key Characteristics of Executive Customer Engagement

Many B2B companies have programs and initiatives that purport to build engagement with executive customers. Typically, however, they are less than successful because they do not meet all of the following six criteria of world-class B2B engagement:

1. *Executive customer participants should represent the top 20 percent of accounts that deliver 80 percent of your revenue.* Look at the list of members in your current or existing market collective and quickly calculate how much revenue they represent. A market collective should only include about 10 to 25 executive customers from those accounts that are most strategically or financially important to your company, division, or geography.

2. *The market collective includes strategic-minded, forward-thinking executive customers and firms.* Every company has executive customers who are "Steady Eddies" or "Laggards." These are loyal customers who have been around forever and often they have a terrific relationship with your company. But if they do not represent a strategic growth opportunity or a substantial volume of revenue, they should not be invited to join the market collective. This is not to say that their loyalty should not be rewarded: be sure to include them when your sales team hands out invitations to golf tournaments and wine tastings, and include them in your customer appreciation programs. But if they are not instrumental to your company's current or future success, do not give them a seat at the table when your company's strategic direction is considered. In all likelihood, that conversation wouldn't even be relevant to them.

Think about the leading companies in your industry to whom the balance of the industry wants to be connected. This combination of forward-thinking people and companies will elevate the level of contribution significantly.

3. *Participants are all top decision makers within their companies.* As discussed earlier, the members of the market collective should be business leaders within their companies. They should control spending, and they should have significant domain knowledge in your industry and markets.

If you have existing executive customer programs, don't be fooled by their names. We often see B2B companies whose "Executive Councils" are composed of end users and managers, who are not empowered to make high-dollar purchase decisions. In fact, it is a good idea to check the titles of the participants in all your customer programs, especially respondents to satisfaction surveys.

As we've seen in the B2B world, user satisfaction does not equate to spending as directly as it does in the B2C world. There is no substitute for understanding and engaging the person who signs the contracts.

As one CEO shared, "At first we just got warm bodies and weren't picky about the level of the participants, and it was like a focus group. Once we stepped it up to true decision makers, the strategic value to our team shot through the roof."

4. *The program focuses on gathering collective insight, rather than individual opinions about your company.* There have been countless books written and consulting practices developed around the power of collective brainstorming and synergistic thinking. Imagine unleashing that power when you have the group of decision makers who control your fate in one room. The wealth of ideas that surface from those who control a substantial portion of your company's revenues cannot be overemphasized. Working together they form a bond or allegiance to a collective cause—the success of your business!

Meeting collectively also gives some level of market validation or evaluation of ideas. The ideas of individual customers can be immediately validated based on the responses of the rest of the collective. You want to know as quickly as possible if an issue or viewpoint raised by one customer is shared across the market. If the response from the collective indicates that it does, your team can safely consider investing time and resources pursuing it. Conversely, if the response tells you the issue is either isolated or not compelling enough to command their attention as a group, you will need to temper your investment accordingly, or simply deal with it at an account level.

Individual meetings with your top customers are critical, but they do not replace the foundation of developing your market collective, which you will use to formulate and validate strategy and enhance relationships.

5. ***The market collective connects directly to the leadership team.*** Remember the child's game "Telephone"? In this game, a message starts at one end of the line and is whispered between each player until it reaches the other end. How often is the message the same at the end as it was at the beginning? Almost never. In the repeated retellings, the message is misheard, misinterpreted, and misspoken. Communication in the business world transpires very similarly. How often does a decision-making executive hear information first-hand from the source? More likely, decisions are based upon a presentation of data that has been collected, interpreted, perhaps spun, and formulated into conclusions by many "Telephone" players down the line.

When you connect a market collective directly to your leadership team, you ensure that everyone on the team hears the message at the same time. Sure, some of your team members will still hear it differently or try to massage or reinterpret it, but the rest of the team will have heard the original message and that will keep everyone honest. This is another reason why connecting directly to executive customers is so powerful a tool compared to other means of gathering market information, such as focus groups and analyst reports. Without a doubt, these latter techniques can be useful, but the information that the leadership team hears is not firsthand; it has been interpreted and retold many times. Nothing beats your team hearing the direct words from a group of decision makers drawn from your most important customer accounts.

6. *Interaction with the collective is face-to-face.* Lastly, hearing information first-hand also means meeting face-to-face. This aspect of executive customer engagement cannot be ignored. In today's world of telecommuting and virtual work, it is tempting to try to get by with phone calls, video conferences, and email. But these are not the right ways to develop relationships with and gain the trust and confidence of people to whom you will entrust your company's future. Executive customers merit quality time with you and they should get to know you as well as possible.

Finally, if you don't meet face-to-face, you and your team will miss important nuances that are only visible when you can see a speaker and the reactions of others to his or her words. And by the way, when you are trying to build relationships and create an emotional bond, mixing in a little fun doesn't hurt either.

The above six criteria *must* be met to successfully engage executive customers. Missing even one element means you may not be talking to the right people or that your leadership team may be missing important information. There is no point in forfeiting the effectiveness of an executive customer initiative by compromising it from the start.

Executive Customer Advisory Councils: The Playbook Cornerstone

The most effective kind of market collective and the best foundation for larger executive customer initiatives is the executive customer advisory council (ECAC, or councils). These councils provide a single reference point for a B2B company's leadership team, including its functional heads. We believe so strongly in the council's ability to transform B2B business that we call it the cornerstone of the entire *Playbook*.

Imagine having your entire leadership team, including functional heads, tethered to a single reference point—and that one reference point is a group of 10 to 25 true decision makers from your most important customers. Once or twice a year, they gather offsite to discuss developments in their industries, markets, companies, and specific areas of responsibility. After a day or two of intimate interaction with these top customers, the event is followed up with ongoing engagement and discussion through subcommittees and other forums and communication.

ECAC meetings have a transformative effect on leader-to-leader relationships both externally and internally. The executive customers who attended the meeting now seek *you* out because you provided such a valuable forum for them to network and learn from their peers. They want to do more. They have become part of your team.

In turn, the leaders in the host company hear customers candidly discussing their challenges, aspirations, and priorities firsthand. They learn how the company's executive customers think and make decisions—as well as how their business environment is changing and what they are doing to address it. The leadership team gains critical insight into key questions, such as:

- Where is the market going?

- How are the customer's companies evolving?

- What are customers' needs and priorities?

- How are customers addressing their challenges and aspirations?

- How could the host company better work with and help customers?

Exhibit 4-1: Executive Customer Advisory Councils typically consist of group sessions, breakout sessions, and time for networking

ECACs provide B2B companies with an opportunity to see the world through the eyes of the professionals who will ultimately decide how their resources and dollars will be allocated. As $72 million industrial business unit president Tom Furey of Standard Register shares, "Our inaugural council meeting validated our relevance in the market and highlighted the opportunities to partner at the executive level with our top customers. Having our leadership team experience this together had an impact that would have never been achieved otherwise. It has transformed how we think and changed the way we plan and lead moving forward."

Understanding ECACs

As we work with B2B companies, we find that their perceptions of market collectives vary wildly. Often, any group of customers that has an affiliation with a B2B seller—from user groups to focus groups to online communities to panels—is called advisory council. True councils adopt the following structural and operational parameters:

Objective and Purpose: To provide B2B leaders with direct input from the highest levels of their customer base regarding market and customer trends, priorities, and direction. This input enables better decision making regarding strategy, positioning, competitive responses, and the evaluation of potential partners and acquisitions. The ECAC's ultimate purpose is to provide and capture greater value in the markets served by B2B companies.

Internal Team Roster: ECACs are led by the owner of the host company's P&L. This individual is usually the CEO or the head of a business unit or subsidiary. The ECAC leader should also be the executive sponsor of the company's or business unit's executive customer initiative, which means he or she will be its champion and be accountable for its success. Other internal members of the ECAC should include the go-to-market leadership team, including the executive sponsor's direct reports in finance, marketing, R&D, sales, service, and strategy. The internal team may also include the Board of Directors, who often attend ECAC meetings as guests and observers.

External Membership Roster: The customer members of councils are the final decision makers from a B2B's most important customers. In IT companies, such as Oracle, HCL Technologies, and Intel, they are usually chief information or technology officers (CIOs or CTOs). In publishing companies, such as Springer Science+Business

Media, they are the heads of large library systems and major booksellers. In logistics companies, such as Intesource, they are procurement
heads and chief financial officers (CFOs).

Discussion: ECAC dialogue is focused on securing input or
feedback on operational and strategic business issues. It is not presen-
tation-driven or sales-focused. Instead, the internal team should be
facilitating executive customer dialogue and listening far more than
speaking.

Initiative vs. Event: ECACs operate ongoing strategic-level
initiatives in which the interaction with executive customers continues throughout the year. Face-to-face meetings are supplemented with
group calls and committee work.

Development of ECACs is an evolutionary process that takes
place over a number of years. Exhibit 4-2 tracks ECAC development
in three phases.

Exhibit 4-2: The Three Phases of ECAC Development

ECAC Phase 1: First Meeting
Objective
Derive a collective understanding of the customer's world.
• What are executive customers' biggest issues? Why?
• Are customers addressing the issues today? How?
• What issues will customers face in the future? What will customers need to address them?
Message to Customer
Caring: The leadership team of the host company is listening and is taking the time to understand the customers' world.
Results
Executive customers begin to view the host company in new light and open the door to deeper discussions and levels of access.

ECAC Phase 2: Meetings 2 and 3

Objective

Leverage collective understanding of customer's world to identify the biggest opportunities in responding to and assisting with customer issues.

- What solutions can the host company develop to help customers address their current and future issues?
- Which opportunities represent the low-hanging fruit (low risk/high return)?
- How does the market perceive the host company's competencies and competitive differentiators?
- Where are the gaps between the host company's capabilities and the market needs?
- How should the host company prioritize and invest its resources to best respond to customer issues?

Message to Customer

Empowerment: The leadership team is giving executive customers a seat at the leadership table and asking them to help design the company's future.

Results

Executive customers begin to build a stake in the host company and an emotional bond forms.

ECAC Phase 3: Meetings 4 and Beyond

Objective

Obtain ongoing collective guidance to keep company on track and aligned with market

- Strategy: What are the optimal pricing and business models for long-term success?
- R&D: Is the development roadmap progressing in a timely manner and are new solutions properly aligned with customer needs?
- Marketing and Sales: Is the go-to-market strategy on target?
- Service: What are the customers' support needs and how well is the host company providing for those needs?

Message to Customer

Commitment: The leadership team is acting on executive customer advice and direction. It is clear that customers are very important to them.

Results

The bond between executive customers and the host company grows stronger, and the customer perspective is embedded into the company's new offerings, messages, etc. Executive customers begin to become loyal advocates and are willing to increase their participation levels.

The Significance of Emotional Equity

The mini-series/documentary *Band of Brothers* portrays a true story of WWII soldiers, their experiences together, and how their bond still exists decades later. I'm not suggesting that a council's bond is of the same magnitude, but there is a parallel. It's the single best and most consistent way of developing a bond with key accounts for an organization.

At Wells Fargo, one of the council members was getting married and invited the entire council and Wells Fargo executives to the wedding. Wells actually had the council meeting two days prior to the wedding in the same town so all could attend.

At a recent LexisNexis council meeting, the members (leaders from prestigious law schools around the country) actually wrote a song about LexisNexis to the melody of "Windy," by The Association. Their song was about how much they appreciated LexisNexis, how superior the company is to the competition, etc. This was all thought up and written by the members on their own time..As Vice President and law school business unit leader Scott Collins shares, this group has delivered unquestionable strategic value and it feels like a reunion of sorts when they gather. "Everyone appreciates the professional accomplishments and relishes the personal relationships that have been developed," Collins notes. Grace Tonner, Associate Dean at UC Irvine School of Law and LexisNexis Council member shares, "Being on the West Coast, there needs to be a compelling reason for me to travel across three time zones for a day-and-half-meeting. The level of trust, value, and access both professionally and personally has made this one of my career highlights." LexisNexis' Molly Chillinsky has witnessed this level of commitment and contribution over several council initiatives across her organization. She adds, "The combination of value and insight, coupled with the loyalty and bonding is amazing."

In the consumer world, Harley Davidson seems to have won the honor for most committed customers, as thousands have tattooed the Harley Davidson logo on their arms, chest, and backs. While I haven't yet witnessed a council member sporting an Intesource, Wells Fargo,

Crown Partners, Springer, or Oracle tattoo, wedding invitations and customized songs are pretty darn close.

These valuable customers advocate the host organization to prospective customers with a passion and belief like no one else. While this will be covered in great depth in Step 4 of the *Playbook*, it's important to note there is a huge financial return that the emotional bond delivers. They help identify new prospects, drive market awareness, accelerate sales cycles, and close deals.

ECACs in Action: Springer Leaps Ahead

When Springer Science+Business Media looked ahead to the ramifications of the technological revolution in publishing, the company's leaders quickly realized technology had created a new playing field in which the traditional arm's length relationship with customers would disappear. To win in this new environment and capture major gains in terms of opportunities, market share, sales, and margins, Springer needed to adopt the new technology and actively, aggressively, and directly engage customers.

The publisher also recognized the window of opportunity in publishing wouldn't be open for long. It needed to be agile, open to change, and ready to make big bets and investments quickly, but in a calculated fashion. This required the leadership team, the company's board, and indeed, the entire organization to be in agreement on its strategy, as well as aligned with the market. This was accomplished through the formation of a set of regional councils.

Today, Springer has councils composed of executive customers in the corporate, government, medical, and academic sectors. Council meetings are hosted regionally around the world (Korea, Brazil, Vietnam, Dubai, Turkey, U.S., and Portugal) and typically include 16 to 20 top decision makers representing the company's most important customers. The meetings are highly interactive and dialogue-driven around high-level topics such as strategy, product and service innovation, and business models. Council members are very rarely asked to participate in lower-level tasks such as review-

ing product roadmaps or sitting through feature-and-function presentations.

During council meetings, Springer's leadership team typically
seeks insight into market trends and their potential impact on the customer base. These insights help the company identify areas in which it
should invest for mid-term to long-term growth. "This has positioned
us to understand what is happening within our industry and the direction our clients are heading so we can be there when they arrive," says
George Scotti, Springer's vice president of librarian marketing for the
Americas, Europe, the Middle East, and Africa.

Springer's councils have been most useful as springboards for business model transformation. After discovering the broad spectrum of
research needs within its customer base, the company developed and
successfully launched a range of access and pricing models that allow
customers to choose among inclusive, full-access packages, content-
based solutions, and pay-per-view options. "Since 1995, we've been
changing the business model to improve our proposition to libraries,"
explains CEO Derk Haank. "New delivery methods and content access
models have enabled the company to increase the value-to-price ratio
for customers."

For Springer and other B2B companies with which we have
worked, the ability to tap into customer insight through ECACs has
proven enormously valuable. Their market collectives amplify an
"outside-in" or market-driven culture, and they help align the leadership team and drive focus and clarity. The confidence this engenders
among the leaders in a B2B company also accelerates the acceptance
of change and transformation at strategic and operational levels.

Where would Springer be if it had not added key customer decision makers to its team and allowed them to contribute to the company's game plan? "Nowhere near where we are today," declares Syed
Hasan.

CHAPTER 5

PLAN

ALIGNING WITH THE MARKET

*I*n Crown Partners' fifth year, Richard Hearn, its co-founder and CEO, realized the enterprise software company's strategy would not generate the growth and profitability needed to guarantee a sustainable future. Crown's products were successful in the marketplace, but there were too many of them, and few synergies between them.

"Every product we built was a success because we didn't build anything unless we knew we could sell it," Hearn says. "But I knew we had missed some big opportunities by thinking about products individually. Up to that point, we were closing grape-sized deals, but I was sure there were watermelon-sized opportunities out there. Unfortunately, we didn't know what they were or where to find them."

To better align the company with the market and tap into larger sales, Hearn knew he and his leadership team needed to identify, adopt, and execute a fundamentally different strategy. Crown could no longer provide products and services on a one-off basis. It needed to provide broader-based solution suites that could drive much greater value for both Crown and its customers.

"We had to sharpen our vision and how we planned strategically," says Hearn. "We needed to identify not only what was working today, but also what would work over the long term. And that required aligning our internal team before we could move forward." The first step toward aligning Crown's team was securing agreement about the needs and desires of the market. Up to this point, there was plenty of "inside-out" and "we're smart, we can figure this out" thinking. As Hearn recalls, "Our engineers, sales team, product managers, and marketing people all had their own ideas about what our customers wanted. Obviously, not everyone could be right."

Like many B2B companies, Crown tried to resolve these varying visions and find a way forward using a number of conventional strategic planning approaches. Many of them were very complex and academic in application and resulted in frustration, confusion, and more questions than answers.

Two Key Elements of Strategic Planning

The planning approaches Crown Partners tried did not work for two reasons. First, none of them produced a strategic plan that instilled any confidence, clarity, or consensus among the members of the leadership team. Without this internal agreement and accompanying alignment with a specific plan, leadership team members tended to stick to strategies with which they were most familiar, usually those which most closely aligned to their experience and functional perspectives as described in Exhibit 5-1.

Exhibit 5-1: The Functional Perspectives of Strategy

Sales	"Here's what our customers are talking about..." "We need to lower our pricing to gain marketing share." "Here's what we heard at the trade show ..." "Here's why our customers chose the competition... add that feature." "Our biggest customer loves the idea of ..."
Marketing	"Our customer survey results indicate..." "Here's how our focus groups are responding..." "We need to launch a new branding campaign." "Here's what people are saying in our online communities..."
Product Development	"Here are the suggestions from our user conference..." "This new technology will change the game for our products and win us accolades and rewards within the industry and peers..." "If we do X, we will be recognized thought leaders."
Customer Service	"Here's what everyone is calling about..." "These are the common problems our customers are having with our product..." "This is what we are having the most trouble addressing..."
Finance	"The growth in this market doesn't justify the investment." "How do we know they'll buy it?" "This risk far outweighs the potential return."

Source: Geehan Group

The other reason Crown's planning approaches did not work was the lack of speed. Too often, by the time a plan was complete, it was already obsolete. Crown experienced what frustrates thousands of company leaders each year: new competitors, business models, and technologies that spring up in between the beginning and the end of the planning process, which are rarely factored into the resulting strategy. This strategic obsolescence further compromises peace of mind, rightly leaving the leadership team feeling uneasy that the plan is outdated even before it can be executed.

The evolution of television broadcasting technology is an excellent example of the acceleration of industry change (see Exhibit 5-2). For the first 70 years, broadcasting was analog. Then, in the last 10 years, the industry moved from analog to digital to high definition and now to 3-D. Change has gone from nominal to incremental to revolutionary all in a few years, and this acceleration is affecting dozens of other industries.

Exhibit 5-2: Accelerating Change in Television Broadcasting Technology

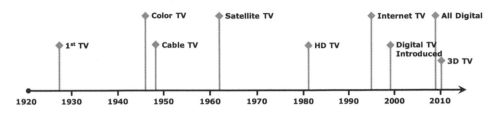

Source: Harris Broadcast Communications Division

The acceleration of change in broadcasting created a barrage of issues at Harris Corporation's Broadcast Communications Division, which supplies technology to the television and video gaming industries. These issues included reduced time-to-market, quality and viewer experience problems, and radical changes in the cost basis of the industry caused by automation and the realignment of business, operational, and content workflows within the major networks and cable companies.

"Our industry was changing so rapidly that we needed to overhaul our planning process to match the velocity of the market," recalls Tim Thorsteinson, former president of the business unit. "We had to make sure we not only kept up, but excelled in meeting our customers' needs and maintaining our ability to compete."

Like Crown Partners and Harris Broadcast, B2B leadership teams need a better strategic planning process—one that is less stressful and frustrating, and much more productive, effective, and confidence-inspiring. A streamlined planning process is not just desirable; it is essential if B2B companies are to match the pace of change in their industries and markets.

A better strategic process should sidestep the politics of compromise and adjustments designed to please internal constituencies. The only compromises allowed should be those required to align the plan with the needs and interests of the market. A better process should also be capable of producing the level of adaptive change required to serve the market. In fast-paced environments, little or no change in a strategic plan is often an indicator of internal resistance to change and opens the doors to competitive threats. Both compromise and change resistance, however, can be avoided when the leadership team has peace of mind regarding strategic direction, corporate priorities, and the levers required to produce SPPG.

Market-Aligned Planning

We call this better approach to strategic planning market-aligned planning (MAP). By now it shouldn't surprise you to read that MAP is closely integrated and synchronized with the activities of executive customer advisory councils. Exhibit 5-3 describes the three stages of the MAP process, its objectives, and key activities.

Exhibit 5-3: Market-Aligned Planning

Market-Aligned Planning

	Input	Evaluate	Validate and Monitor
Objective	Gather the collective input of top executive customers through the ECAC.	Conduct internal evaluation	Plan and confirm strategy with ECAC, monitor execution, review key objectives, and make in-course corrections
Key Activities	ECAC Meeting 1: Leadership team receives collective advice on industry, organization, and function. ECAC reviews internally conducted SWOT analysis	Internal leadership team evaluates input using MAP Venn Diagram. Identifies and weighs key options.	ECAC Meetings 2 and beyond: Leadership team authors, executes, and monitors plan. ECAC validates strategy and offers ongoing feedback and course correction.

Source: Geehan Group

MAP Stage 1: Input

In most strategic planning models, the input that feeds the process is compiled internally by a planning team that uses traditional exercises, such as SWOT (strengths, weaknesses, opportunities, and threats) analysis and data points from industry reports and analyst research. Many organizations also incorporate some customer input into their planning processes, but this input is typically gathered using methods such as voice-of-the-customer surveys, user groups, and focus groups which are aimed at lower levels within customer companies or the customer's customers. These sources of raw material do not provide all the pieces of the strategic planning puzzle.

Executive customer input is the other piece of the puzzle. An effective MAP process requires the higher-level, business-issue perspective of customer decision makers. These executive customers are essential sources in the planning process because they provide information concerning:

- Customer Industry Direction and Trends: the state of the industry as viewed by your customers; where it is going; the key issues, challenges, as well as anticipated changes and their projected impact.

- Customer Business Challenges: the priorities, needs, and aspirations of the ECAC, which provides insight into how customers are allocating their resources to address organizational and industry changes.

- Customer Functional Challenges: the functional priorities, needs, and aspirations of the executive customers to whom you sell (e.g., if you sell to CIOs, an understanding of issues faced by the IT organization).

- Customer Perspective on SWOT: the ECAC's opinion and validation of the host company's biggest strengths, weaknesses, opportunities and threats.

The final point is one many B2B companies miss, often because they are reluctant to share strategic information with customers. But the ECAC members are also trusted members of the leadership team, and their review of the company's strengths and weaknesses offers an invaluable perspective on many elements essential to a sound strategic plan, including:

- Why customers buy from the host company

- What makes the host company unique in customers' eyes

- The strengths of host company's culture

- The viability of its business and service models

- The company's competencies and ability to respond to customers' needs.

It is not necessary to share everything: ECACs don't need to know all of a host company's internal information (such as its cash position, employee morale, turnover, benefits programs, and the condition of its facilities and operational systems), but the perspective of executive customers is needed in key market-facing areas.

Our clients often discover that councils are buying their products and services for very different reasons than was assumed. A few years ago, I sat in an ECAC meeting in which the CEO of a logistics management company confidently summarized the SWOT analysis. "We are so proud that one of our key strengths is our thought leadership position in the market," he said, as he announced a new marketing campaign designed to trumpet this fact. He was shocked when the ECAC nixed the plan, explaining that the host company's two largest competitors spent far more in R&D than its total revenues and published five times as much research.

Why did these executive customers buy from the host company? According to the ECAC, it was because the company was easier to work with, were much more experienced, and its teams were more dependable in completing projects on time and on budget than its competition. This input completely changed the host company's strategy, development, marketing, and sales plans. To the credit of its leadership team, it made the changes and was rewarded by moving from being a niche player (ranked fifth) to the overall leader in its market in just three years.

Councils also play an important role in validating a host company's external opportunities and threats. The collective's input helps B2B companies understand the strategic ramifications of industry shifts, disruptive technologies, regulatory issues, globalization, and the competitive landscape. The greater the insight and clarity a company can muster in these regards, the more effective its strategy plan.

In the same ECAC meeting described above, the CEO of the logistics company also noted that supply chain solutions were low on the company's list of market opportunities. The members of the ECAC disagreed with this placement, stating that supply chain solutions should be among the company's highest priorities because most of them were either investigating or in the process of investing heavily in this area. With this knowledge, the host company re-prioritized its plan. It quickly acquired a best-of-breed supply chain solution company before its competitors even began shopping—saving money on the acquisition and moving into the space 18 months ahead of the industry. The combination of market collectives and SWOT analysis can indeed be a very powerful strategic approach (see Exhibit 5-4).

Exhibit 5-4: Combining Market Collectives and SWOT Analysis

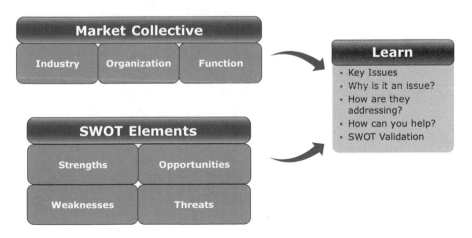

Source: Geehan Group

MAP Stage 2: Evaluate

In the second stage of the MAP process, the planning team takes all the information gathered during in the input stage and plots out its opportunities, priorities, and issues. This stage is designed to ensure that the new strategic plan is anchored in the viewpoints of customers and the market. It also streamlines the planning process by eliminating an overly internal focus, politics, and legacy blinders that create barriers to agile planning.

The Venn diagram is a terrific tool to use in this stage of the MAP process. These diagrams are simple, quick, and effective, and they allow leadership teams to properly position and evaluate input. Typically, companies use Venn diagrams to identify the opportunities that reside at the intersection between two "circles" of strategic input: input regarding their business models ("How do we make money?") and input regarding their core competencies ("What are we good at?"). The problem with this level of analysis is that it doesn't provide a comprehensive strategic view of the business environment; it doesn't include the market perspective provided by executive customers.

Think of it this way: a B2B company can create and execute a strategy aimed at doing what it does best in perfect alignment with its business models and still fail miserably if that strategy is not properly aligned with what executive customers want and will pay for.

This becomes very clear when a third circle representing a B2B company's market collective is added to a Venn diagram (see Exhibit 5-5).

Exhibit 5-5: The Market-Aligned Three-Circle Venn

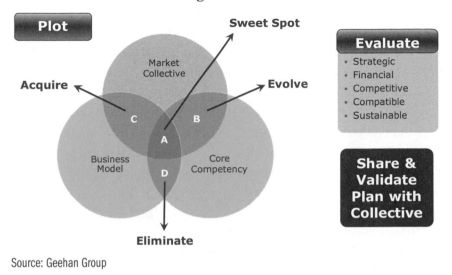

Source: Geehan Group

Adding a third circle composed of data learned from executive customers makes it obvious why strategies that are not market-aligned fail. Look at segment D in Exhibit 5-5. Among other failures, it represents the land of dead-on-arrival products—the B2B's version of B2C's New Coke, Apple's Newton, and the Segway personal transporter. The B2B world has its own share of disappointments, they just aren't as public. How about that new software portal the developers think is cool (but customers don't really need) or the beyond-industry-standard component for which no one will pay the premium price (to cover development and production costs)? The list goes on, and each item on it comes with an enormous price tag.

But let's focus on the silver lining instead of the gray cloud. In addition to those areas where a B2B company should not venture, the MAP Venn diagram in Exhibit 5-5 also identifies the key areas of opportunity.

Three overlapping segments in the Venn diagram represent viable strategic options. First is the "Sweet Spot" represented by Segment A. All three circles intersect here, making this the home of a company's most valuable opportunities. Segments B and C also represent important opportunities because these are options that reflect needs and desires of your customers that do not currently fit either the business model or the competencies of the company. These segments usually harbor unidentified opportunities because they are what customers want and are willing to pay for.

Segments B and C are where we have seen successful B2B companies such as Oracle, Wells Fargo, and Intesource excel and distance themselves from the competition. These two segments present the greatest opportunities for transformation; however, they also require change in what you do (not currently a core competency) or how you operate (currently outside your business model). Therefore, aversion to change is a major reason segments B and C are a source of missed opportunities for B2B companies. But when change is calculated and validated by the market, the investment brings the greatest returns.

Microsoft is becoming less and less relevant to businesses each year because it seems it cannot access the opportunities in Segments B and C in a reliable and timely manner. Why not? Through the lens of B2B best practices, I find the company too focused on end users, which affects both its product/service set, as well as its business model. As a result, Microsoft has been late to enter emerging markets, such as mobile and cloud computing, and is behind on business models such as pay-as-you-go as Salesforce.com operates. As a result, the company is losing its edge in the B2B arena.

Segment A is the Sweet Spot: Ideas residing in Segment A represent strategy options consistent with a B2B company's business model, its capabilities, and the needs of its customers. This sweet spot is where a company's efforts should already be focused or where it is heading with all its plans, priorities, and investments.

> *"Engaging our leadership team in meaningful discussions with groups of senior-level customers has unquestionably driven our strategy, internal alignment, and priorities."*

–Jeb Dasteel, Chief Customer Officer, Oracle

Segment B requires business model evolution: Segment B contains the opportunities a B2B company's top customers want, it has the capabilities to produce, but its current business model does not yet support. The problem may be as simple as an incongruity within pricing structure. For example, a company may have a per-item pricing model when customers actually prefer a bundled price option, or bill by the hour when customers want the security and budgeting efficiency of a flat project rate. Whatever the missing piece, companies need to pursue either incremental or breakthrough evolution in their business models to capture the opportunities in Segment B.

Consider Microsoft once more. The company has great software that business customers find stable, users are familiar with, and for which support is available around the globe. But their traditional business model dictated that customer companies buy this software for an up-front fixed fee and load it onto their servers. One of these programs is a customer relationship management (CRM) program embedded in the email application, Outlook, that allows salespeople and marketers to manage their interactions with customers. So far, so good.

Then comes Salesforce.com, a small start-up that offers a similar CRM solution with an innovative business model. The Salesforce.com model requires no software (or IT staff); it is accessed via the Internet. There is no up-front license charge; instead, customers pay a monthly fee based on the number of users. And while Microsoft only offers one-size-fits-all CRM software, Salesforce.com encourages external developers to write applications customers can use to integrate and customize its service. Is it any surprise that Salesforce.com now has annual revenues exceeding $1 billion?

This is just one of the battles Microsoft is fighting in B2B markets; others include operating systems (Linux), computing processing optimization (VMware, Citrix), and mobile computing (Blackberry, Apple, Google). We can't predict the names of the winners, but we can tell you it will surely be the company that best meets the needs of their executive customers.

Segment C requires development and/or capability acquisition: Segment C in the market-aligned Venn diagram includes opportunities B2B executive customers want and are consistent with the company's business model, but for which the company lacks the capability to deliver. Like all opportunities surfaced in the Venn diagram, the size of these opportunities varies. They could be a simple line extension or addition of a support service to a current offering, an entirely new product category, or entry into a new geographic market.

A B2B company has three choices in considering Segment C opportunities: it can develop the competency internally, buy it, or seek an external partner who has it. Line extensions and supplemental offerings can typically be done internally. Adding services to your portfolio which are outside your current competency usually requires partnering or buying and assimilating the offering into your organization. Adding entire categories generally requires an acquisition.

Take the example of a law firm that specializes in international business. Prospering with the rise of globalization over the last few years, more and more of the firm's clients began expanding their R&D operations into emerging nations such as China and India. This trend created an enormous opportunity for the firm to offer counsel and services that secure and protect the intellectual property (IP) of its largest and best clients. But the firm did not have this capability, and the demand grew very quickly. In response, the firm acquired an existing IP law firm and gained immediate expertise and credibility in this category.

This is a common story that can be seen in any industry. In the IT industry, hardware-focused Dell purchased Perot Systems to extend its competencies in IT services instead of growing its own global IT service company. Hewlett-Packard did the same when it purchased EDS, as did Xerox when it acquired ACS.

Segment D requires pruning: The final segment in the market-aligned Venn diagram is where many companies stumble. Why do so many new products fail? Because many of them represent opportunities for which companies have a capability and a business model, but there is no market demand. This can happen for a number of reasons, including:

1. *Input was limited to the end user:* As we've seen, the end user perspective tends to drive incremental innovation, such as adding features and functions to an existing product or service. But while these enhancements may be useful, do they actually provide business value to customer companies? And are executive customers willing to pay a premium to cover their development costs and provide the necessary return to the B2B seller?

2. *Internal special projects:* Too often, companies pursue opportunities because an executive or someone in R&D has the power or the passion to commandeer funding. The problem, of course, is that proof-of-concept has been ignored and the project has not been vetted by the market.

3. *Innovation races:* Clayton Christensen, the Harvard Business School professor and innovation guru, calls this trap "performance oversupply." Companies fall into it when they are so intent on meeting every advance their competitors make that they outrun their customers. The result is solutions that are technologically superior with no markets.

Pursuing opportunities in Segment D not only results in wasted time and resources, it erodes the credibility of a B2B company in the marketplace. Corporate customers don't look kindly on overblown promises and solutions that miss their mark. The resulting failures also create a downward spiral in terms of morale, pride, focus, and business results inside B2B companies.

We find that the first time most B2B companies create a market-aligned Venn diagram, it reveals that 20 percent to 40 percent of their current R&D resources are flowing to Segment D. The best course of action is to weed out these questionable projects as soon as possible. Close them down or sell them off and re-channel the resources they have been consuming to opportunities that excite executive customers. This exercise revealed rather quickly to the Crown leadership team the strategy necessary to meet revenue growth targets. Hearn will tell you he felt confident sunsetting his Segment D projects since key executive customer decision makers advised him it was the right thing to do (see Exhibit 5-6).

Exhibit 5-6: Crown Partners Plots Its Strategy Using the Market-Aligned Venn Diagram

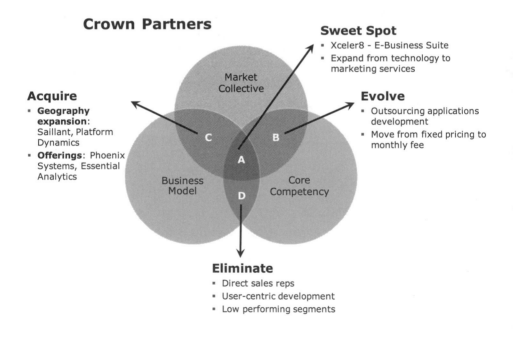

You may also take a lesson from Harris Broadcast: "Our council's perspectives, desires, and ideas gave us the courage to eliminate offerings we have held onto for too long, and narrow our priorities to the offerings that helped them the most," recalls Tim Thorsteinson. "This approach catapulted our market position and value with customer decision makers." Harris was then able to reallocate those dollars and people to more relevant and game changing opportunities (see Exhibit 5-7).

Exhibit 5-7: Harris Broadcast Market-Aligned Venn Diagram

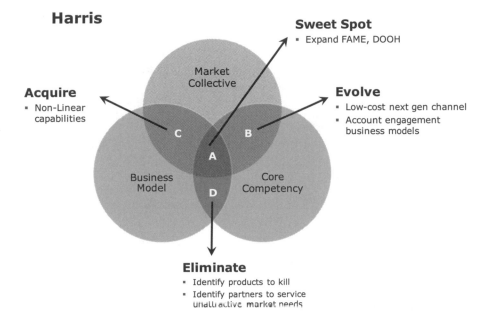

MAP Stage 3: Validate & Monitor

Once a B2B company has completed the first two stages of the MAP process, it can author and execute its strategic plan. The first thing companies that use this process notice is authoring the plan is surprisingly fast and easy. That's because the market collective creates a filter for eliminating the frustrating, unproductive, and divisive behaviors that bog down the conventional strategic process. Further, when it's time to convince a board of directors to accept a plan that calls for major investments, acquisitions, or shifts in direction, it is much easier when they have already heard directly from the company's biggest customers.

Armed with insights and rigorous analysis, the final elements of the MAP process are straightforward. They include:

1. *Destination:* Determine where you are going (Sweet Spots, Evolve, Acquire).

2. *Plan:* Outline how you are going to get there (priortization and resource allocation).

3. *Execute and Monitor:* Determine critical success factors, key metrics, and accountablilty.

4. *Continuous ECAC Input:* Keep your market collective engaged throughout the entire journey.

B2B companies should be careful not to overburden their ECACs during this final stage of strategic planning. Instead, they should determine where the council's input is most valuable and avoid going to its members for input on issues that don't pertain to them. As long as this rule is followed, executive customers will freely share their time and expertise.

That said, B2B companies should tap their ECACs for input on market-facing issues. In R&D, that can include the design and integration of solutions at the user, operational, and business levels. In marketing, that can include the value proposition, messaging, and campaign development and review. In sales, that can include business case, selling process, and price setting and structure. In service, it can include what and how much support to offer, and whether and how to charge for it.

B2B companies should also seek validation from their ECACs at key points in the MAP process. If they aren't included, executive customers won't have a chance to refine and review their own ideas. Like anyone else, executive customers can change their minds over time in response to shifts in their industries and markets. Continuous validation ensures that executive customers have a chance to reappraise and refine their input, and this can help avoid costly mistakes. Oracle, for example, validates everything from development plans to industry trends and directions to potential acquisition ideas with its market collectives.

Including top customer decision makers in the B2B planning process ensures their fingerprints are all over the strategic plan. Their participation creates emotional equity in the plan for them, as well as emotional equity for the internal leadership team who will be charged with supporting and executing it. Input of executive customers also provides confidence to the leadership team to undertake major decisions, such as entering a new business or divesting assets that are no longer a good fit.

I'll close this chapter with one final market-aligned Venn, this time from Wells Fargo.

Exhibit 5-8: Wells Fargo Identifies Key Strategies Through Market-Aligned Planning

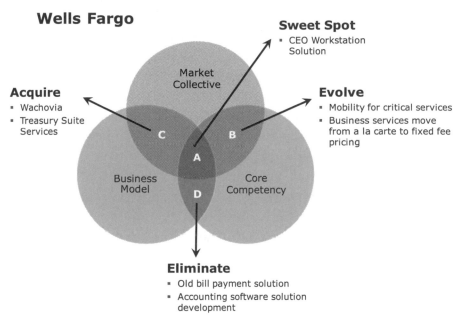

CHAPTER 6

COLLABORATE

ELEVATING RELATIONSHIPS AND
UNLEASHING INNOVATION

"Turn on a television or a radio almost anywhere in the world, and chances are good that the signal you receive is being broadcast with hardware made and sold by Harris Corporation's Broadcast Communications Division."[1]

Harris's roots in broadcasting go back to Gates Radio, which introduced the radio transmitter in the 1930s. As the radio industry grew, local stations like WLW in Cincinnati, WJR in Detroit, and WOR in New York needed powerful systems to transmit their signals farther and farther over the airwaves. They all used Gates equipment. In 1957, Harris acquired Gates to gain the leverage needed to enter the newly emerging market in television broadcasting.

Harris's VHF and UHF transmitters drove the company's growth as television boomed in the 1950s and 1960s. Throughout the 1980s and 1990s, however, the broadcast market evolved on two fronts. As the market matured, broadcast transmission became a low-margin business. At the same time, the broadcaster's world became more complex. Broadcasters were challenged to drive ad sales and deliver newer, faster, and more dynamic content to a widening distribution network. To keep up with these changes in its markets, Harris Broadcast went on a buying spree. Between 1997 and 2007, the division acquired 11 companies around the world and positioned itself as an industry leader.

---

[1] Harris Broadcast Website

But the leaders of the broadcast division knew trouble was brewing. Its acquisitions and varied product and service portfolios turned Harris into a siloed organization. There were a dozen different product and service lines with separate P&Ls. Engineers, developers, marketers, and sales reps were all focused on the one category they knew best. Very few of them had a clear understanding of the overall value of Harris's offerings, the gaps that existed among them, how they could be integrated, and most importantly, how to leverage customer relationships to market and sell across all of them.

In 2008, as Tim Thorsteinson, who was president of the $584 million broadcast division at the time, considered how to integrate the business unit's portfolios and break down the silos, he realized he needed a more detailed and intimate understanding of the needs and directions of its top customers. He also knew the division's account teams would need a much higher level of business acumen and executive presence if they were to successfully sell an integrated portfolio of offerings. To address these needs and gain the insight needed to guide the division forward, Thorsteinson launched an ECAC, whose membership included the technology leaders from the division's best broadcasting and media customers.

At the first meeting of the ECAC, the leadership team at Harris Broadcast received a huge wake-up call. Members of the market collective made it clear Harris customer-facing teams didn't have a deep enough understanding of their customers' operating environments or possess the customer relationships necessary to turn the monumental changes that were taking place in the industry into growth opportunities. However, several of the ECAC members became so impressed with the expanded capabilities the division had acquired, they invited Harris's executives to continue discussions with their companies individually to help address key issues they were facing. A perfect opportunity had surfaced: Harris Broadcast needed to deepen its relationships with executive customers, had capabilities the market needed and wanted, and those very same customers were inviting the company in to learn from each other and to collaborate on issues that would keep Harris a market leader.

To capitalize, the division's executives first began working one-on-one with top decision makers in its customer companies to help them address their business issues. In the process, the company began to elevate its status from a vendor to that of a trusted advisor, and in some cases, business partner with executive customers. Second, it identified opportunities to co-develop solutions for individual custom-ers that could be monetized across the market at a significant margin. Harris Broadcast transformed its relationships with executive custom-ers into an innovation engine capable of driving SPPG. This is the powerful source of innovation that is produced in the third step in *The B2B Executive Playbook*.

Supercharging Customer Relationships

Step 3 takes a B2B company's relationships with executive customers to a deeper, one-on-one level. It is designed to cultivate *collaboration* between a B2B seller and its top customer companies in order to foster customer loyalty and dependence, as well as innovation and SPPG.

Customer loyalty and dependence are hot topics in business today because they drive customer retention rates. Retaining existing customers costs less to sell and service than winning new customers. And that means higher margins.

In the B2C world, customer dependence comes in the form of preference. Consumer package goods companies, for example, spend the bulk of their marketing dollars on brand awareness, pricing advan-tages, focus groups, packaging, and gaining access to consumers. This leads to long-running brand wars in which battles are won or lost in tenths of percentage points of market share. Think of Coke versus Pepsi, Crest versus Colgate, and Revlon versus Cover Girl.

In the B2B world, however, where companies have relatively few customers, customer dependence is built on one-on-one relationships that encourage continuous engagement and open access. It begins with relationships with key decision makers and then expands down through the entire customer organization.

The best of these relationships are symbiotic—the B2B company and the customer company become *interdependent*. The success of both parties is based upon an alliance characterized by mutual engagement, understanding, and alignment that is rooted in the needs, challenges, and aspirations of both parties.

As such a relationship develops, a B2B company becomes more and more an indispensible source of products and services that its customers need in order to capture value in their businesses. The more significant and positive the effects of these solutions on the customer's business, the greater the customer's reliance on the seller.

General Electric Aviation and Boeing provide a good example of an interdependent relationship. Whether it is speed, fuel efficiency, range, payload, maintenance, etc., the ultimate success of a Boeing plane is highly dependent on the capability and performance of the engine provided by GE Aviation. Each company needs the other to maximize its success. They are interdependent.

Although Boeing and GE are among the world's largest companies, the size of a B2B company does not matter when it comes to creating an interdependent relationship with customers. For instance, when the largest companies in the world are involved in a major merger or acquisition, they often enlist the services of Wachtell, Lipton, Rosen & Katz. The law firm has only one office and 200 lawyers, a fraction of the several thousand lawyers and dozens of offices around the globe that the largest firms boast. Yet for the past nine years, Wachtell has been the highest revenue and profit generator per attorney of any law firm in the world; profits per partner in 2010 were $4.3 million. The firm has also been named the most prestigious law firm to work for in the world several years in a row.

Instead of billing by the hour, like virtually every other law firm, Wachtell simply sends a very large invoice at the end of a project based on what its partners think it is owed. These invoices reportedly cause even the largest companies to take pause, but Wachtell's legal guidance delivers an unquestionable competitive advantage and financial impact. As a result, the firm commands premium fees, and is consistently the most profitable law firm in the world. By the way, those fees don't go for marketing: the firm's website, for example, has no slick designs or flash videos. It's composed of about 12 pages of plain text and an employee directory. This is the power of becoming a business partner in the minds of your customers.

The B2B Relationship Continuum

As discussed in Chapter 2, the relationships B2B companies have with their customers fall into five basic categories along a continuum which is organized by:

1. The level of value the customer places upon a supplier, and

2. The impact the supplier has on the customer's success.

Exhibit 6-1: The B2B Relationship Continuum

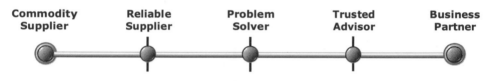

| Commodity Supplier | Reliable Supplier | Problem Solver | Trusted Advisor | Business Partner |

Source: Geehan Group

The higher the level of value you provide your customer, the farther along the continuum executive customers will place your company. Greater margins come with positions closer to the right of the continuum.

When evaluating what position on the B2B Relationship Continuum a company enjoys with a customer, it is important to remember that the value of the relationship is solely determined by the customer. This may appear obvious, but many companies have unrealistic or just flat-out wrong ideas about how they are perceived by customers. These misperceptions explain the befuddlement that B2B executives feel when customers they thought were *loyal* (usually because they have been customers for years) disappear at the first lower bid. When a B2B company loses a customer on price, it is highly likely that the customer thought of the company as a commodity supplier or reliable supplier, and no more.

Exhibit 6-2: B2B Customer Relationship Assessment

Commodity Supplier	Reliable Supplier	Problem Solver	Trusted Advisor	Business Partner
You are a Commodity Supplier if...	**You are a Reliable Supplier if...**	**You are a Problem Solver if...**	**You are a Trusted Advisor if...**	**You are a Business Partner if...**
...you lunch with a purchasing agent, and you have his office phone number. In most cases, your bids are responses to an RFP (Request for Proposal) developed by someone to whom you have limited or no access.	...you usually start with purchasing, but you can get meetings with influencers in order to prepare them for a meeting with their bosses (the decision maker).	...influencers and decision makers exhibit a sense of immediacy when they ask to meet with you. They have your cell number and call when a specific situation arises.	...you lunch with the person who has been tasked with solving a problem and he or she has engaged you to address it. You have his or her cell phone number, and the customer often calls you for advice and input.	...you lunch with a decision maker who is specifically engaged and sponsors your company to help solve complex, mission-critical business issues. You are the only company that offers a solution that gives your customers a key point of differentiation, competitive advantage, unique capability, or delivers business results they could not achieve without you.
Your company works through **purchasing** or competes in a bidding process each time its contract expires. The customer considers your products and services a commodity wherein price, not value, is the primary and sometimes the only criteria.	You have preferred access to the purchasing department, often because you have topical material and information they need.	Your company has infrequent contact with influencers and few critical interactions with decision makers. Deals are highly dependent on specific events, situations, or shifts in the customer's business environment.	You have ongoing access to **influencers** but limited interaction with decision makers. In many cases, the **decision maker** has asked you to help them design the next RFP that has many add-on opportunities. You may be the only supplier contacted.	You share the investment in the development and implementation of a product or service. You also share in the outcome of the success and/or failure.
Caution: Just because a purchasing or lower-level manager asks your company for help on an RFP, doesn't mean that you have a valued relationship. Often, they are simply leveraging your knowledge, and still view you as a commodity vendor.				
Phone call test: If you call your executive customer's administrative assistant and the response is "Who are you and what is your call regarding please...?"	**Phone call test:** If you call the influencer, the admin needs specifics on why you need to meet or talk. They will get back to you if a meeting or call is necessary. "Just send the information over for review" is a common response.	**Phone call test:** If you call the admin and are put right through to your contact due to temporary circumstances; otherwise you are treated like a Reliable Supplier.	**Phone call test:** When you call, the admin openly shares the decision maker's schedule and availability. The admin knows who you are and doesn't require a reason to put you through.	**Phone call test:** You have the decision maker's cell phone, and when you call the office, the admin asks, "How soon do you need to see her?" or "How much time do you need?"

Source: Geehan Group

It is well worth taking a moment to assess the position of your company's relationships with your key customers. Reading the descriptions in Exhibit 6-2, how do you think the decision makers in customer companies view your company? If you need help, use the phone call test at the bottom of each column. It is a surprisingly quick and accurate gauge of how a customer views your company.

It is uncommon for B2B companies to achieve the status of business partner with all its major customers, but they should try to move to the right of the Relationship Continuum whenever possible. The ability to do this is also dependent on a company's product and service portfolio. Obviously, if a customer is buying something that is a widely available commodity, it is more difficult to move to the right of the continuum than if the product or service is highly differentiated. In the former case, however, collaborating with customers to drive innovation can be a B2B company's ticket to enhancing its relationship with the customer and capturing revenue and margin growth.

Dell provides a good example. After years of computer hardware becoming more of a commodity, Dell acquired more than a dozen companies with the aim of enhancing its position on the Relationship Continuum. While traditional hardware companies fall between Commodity and Reliable Supplier on the lower end, mid-range software companies and services fall on the higher end between Problem Solver and Trusted Advisor, and even up to Business Partner. This is why Dell made software acquisitions (Compellent Technologies, EqualLogic) and service acquisitions (Perot Systems, Boomi).

Institutionalize Key Account Relationships

Although building relationships with individual decision makers is very important, it is vital to create relationships at higher levels in key functional areas of the company as well as the corporation. Developing *institutional relationships* is the only way to weather personnel changes, and ensure stability and longevity of customer relationships.

When the relationship includes multiple people and groups, your customers are much less likely to take their business to the competitor, and your employees are less likely to take your customers with them to their next employer. Is your customer dependent upon you, your B2B company and its products, or to Bob, your sales superstar? If your answer is Bob, then imagine the revenue loss when Bob leaves your company and takes the account to a competitor. The only way to mitigate this risk is to institutionalize the relationship, or make sure Bob is not the sole reason your customer stays with you. You want your customers to stay because they are part of and loyal to your company as a collective institution.

The first step towards building loyalty beyond an individual often begins functionally. For example, companies who have multiple facilities and real estate in many locations have outsourced the majority of the day-to-day upkeep and maintenance to facilities management companies. Some of these facilities management companies started out as office cleaning services (commodity), but expanded their offerings (maintenance, real estate negotiations, security, construction, etc.) to achieve Business Partner at the functional level (operations or facilities management) and Problem Solver to the entire organization. By adding more valuable offerings, the facilities management service company increased its overall relevancy and value to the customer. Each move to the right delivered greater margin and predictability. Harris has done the same by continuing to acquire higher-value offerings as older technologies mature.

Effective B2B collaboration builds relationships at the high-end of the Relationship Continuum across both institutions. In most instances, this collaboration accomplishes together what neither organization could on its own. It takes the relationship to the next level. It redefines the relationship.

Let's look at how to build it.

Account-Based Innovation

The most effective means of taking B2B customer relationships to the level of business partner is through the collaborative power of *Account-Based Innovation* (ABI). ABI provides a platform to advance customer relationships along the Relationship Continuum and expand a B2B company's solution portfolio.

As we saw with Harris Broadcast, the opportunity to pursue ABI with individual executive customers is typically a natural by-product of interactions with the members of a market collective as developed through an Executive Customer Advisory Council. As ECAC members gain a more intimate understanding of a B2B company, trust and credibility is strengthened, and the door to greater involvement is opened. Further, with these executive customer relationships established and the market collective's input as a reference point, a B2B company is ready to do a deep dive with individual executive customers. These sessions are aimed at uncovering specific issues and opportunities that can deliver outsized value to the customer and, in the best cases, can also be launched in the broader marketplace.

At Harris Broadcast, this is exactly what happened after its first ECAC meeting. Upon hearing executive customers talk about problems and issues of which the division had not been aware, its leadership saw the opportunity to learn much more about each customer's unique aspirations for the future and the role that Harris could play in providing greater value to those marquee accounts. Better yet, since these executive customers represented companies that were highly influential in their industries (in some instances, determining industry protocols and standards), the leadership team reasoned that any value it produced for them would be of interest to the market at large. They were right.

> **"Our ABI program completely redefined our longstanding customer relationships in ways we had never before witnessed."**
>
> —Brian Cabeceiras, Vice President, Strategy and Marketing
> Harris Broadcast Communications

The Benefits of ABI

ABI's focus on mutual value makes it more credible with customers and more effective in achieving results than conventional key account programs, such as strategic account management, major account programs, and account-based marketing. In addition to delivering the sales-related objectives typical of these programs, ABIs also provide these additional benefits where most traditional account programs fall short:

- Customers stretch how you think about your business

- R&D is provided with built-in testers, case studies, and testimonials

- Heightened customer visibility, credibility, access, and retention within customer companies

- Increase of sole-source sales (only your company is asked to provide the service so no bidding war) and up-selling opportunities

Customers Stretch Your Thinking

Most B2B companies have vast amounts of intellectual depth and property. The challenge for many companies is to figure out how to connect the right people inside their organizations with the right people in customer companies in order to produce new solutions that couldn't have been achieved otherwise. This is why it is often useful to bring together representatives from the R&D teams of the host and customer companies in ABI programs. Joint brainstorming and problem-solving sessions can generate results that neither party could have accomplished alone.

When you work in close collaboration with customers and share details about one another's needs and capabilities, the joint brainstorming and problem-solving sessions naturally lead to ideas that would not have surfaced in normal circumstances (see Exhibit 6-3).

Exhibit 6-3: Value-Driven Dialogue from ABI Programs

Customer	B2B Seller
• "Have you thought about doing this? • "I know you think this is what you're great at, but I think it's actually ..." • "What if your pricing model offered ...?" • "Why couldn't we simply outsource that to your firm?"	• "We have this best practice that we could leverage for you." • "We could assign a team of engineers to build that capability."

Source: Geehan Group

Certainly that has been the case for $148 million Henny Penny Corporation, a family-owned manufacturer of food service equipment. "Account-based innovation programs are the backbone of our organization's culture and success," says President Rob Connelly. "We work extremely close with our top customers. Our design and engineering teams share ideas, collaborating to provide new solutions, solve problems, or change the game."

One of the home runs at Henny Penny was the development of revolutionary low oil volume (LOV) fryer for McDonald's Corporation. With the cost of cooking oil skyrocketing, McDonald's challenged Henny Penny to design a fryer that used almost half the oil of the fryers then on the market. "We'd been studying innovative ways of improving shortening usage in the frying process for quite awhile," recalls Connelly. "But together with McDonald's, we developed a breakthrough product, which not only yields significant cost savings, but is also easy to operate and minimizes environmental impact."

The LOV fryer earned Henny Penny the prestigious McDonald's Global Innovation Award in 2008. In 2009, McDonald's named Henny Penny Worldwide Equipment Supplier of the Year and in 2010, Worldwide Equipment Partner of the Year. That kind of market clout and credibility can't be bought—and it led to even more sales. In addition to sales opportunities at McDonald's 30,000 restaurants worldwide, Henny Penny applied these innovations to stock models successfully rolled out to the small and mid-sized restaurant marketplace.

Henny Penny also scored a huge hit with KFC, with its innovative warming cabinet design, earning them Yum! Brands' coveted Star Award and KFC's Supplier of the Year Award for 2010. Connelly shares, "Being recognized by industry giants speaks to the continued focus on outstanding, individualized product innovation that stems from every level of the Henny Penny organization."

R&D with Built-in Testers, Case Studies, and Testimonials

It is very common for customer companies engaged in ABI programs to provide resources to help test and refine solutions, as well as share their stories with others in the industry. With this vested interest and buy-in (as well as investment) in co-designing solutions, the risk of innovation failure is much lower with projects derived from ABI programs. According to an executive at a large technology company, "When executive customers are embedded into the development process, they would have to be schizophrenic not to help promote the success they help build."

Crown Partners worked closely with one of its customers to co-design a solution that was very successful. Afterwards, an executive from the company shared his experience with a group of peers at an industry event. The executive customer's endorsement of Crown went far beyond a typical, mechanical recommendation. In fact, the audience could sense there was something special about Crown, and, as a result, the company secured a significant amount of work from other executives at the event. "There is no way that our telling this story would have had 5 percent of the impact this executive had," says Crown CEO Richard Hearn.

Heightened Customer Visibility, Credibility, Access, and Retention

When a B2B company is sponsored by and collaborating directly with a customer, the chances of that customer buying services from another company or even bidding the work out is drastically reduced. ABI programs raise the customer's view of the company's offering from a cost-and-functionality perspective, to the plane of mutual business value. This is an advantaged position for any B2B company.

At Crown Partners, for instance, ABI programs provided opportunities to collaborate and develop solutions with executive customers who were located two to three levels higher in customer companies than anyone the company had worked with previously. By working on the issues important to the highest levels of customer companies, a B2B company's relevance and exposure creates an opportunity to improve its position on the Relationship Continuum. Crown Partners' ABI programs helped the company go from being virtually unknown in its markets and working through purchasing and responding to RFPs, to becoming a known entity at the decision-maker level and being invited into key discussions much earlier and at much higher levels of customer organizations. This exposure solidified the customer relationship at the corporate level and resulted in higher retention levels.

Increase of Sole-source Sales and Up-selling Opportunities

Plain and simple, ABI programs bolster sales. First, they promote sole-source contracts that shut out competitors. After Intesource connected with its executive customers, a CFO at one company phoned CEO Tom Webster about a serious problem he was having with his balance sheet. Webster initially thought the problem was outside his company's realm, but the customer was convinced Intesource had the capabilities needed to solve it, and indeed it did. Intesource earned a sole-source sale, enhanced a customer relationship, and created a profitable new service that could be sold to other customers.

Second, ABI programs create valuable up-selling opportunities. Most B2B companies provide many more products and services than their customers know about. This is particularly true in companies that are transforming themselves from product to solutions companies, making acquisitions, or are very well known for only one or two of their offerings. An ABI host executive at Harris Broadcast discovered such an opportunity during a Friday afternoon meeting with a customer. The customer mentioned an RFP was closing on Monday for a solution he thought Harris could not provide. In fact, Harris could, and hearing this, the customer assigned members of his team to help Harris's staff complete its proposal over the weekend. Harris was able to extend the RFP due date and submit a proposal for a major deal in three days.

In all the ways discussed above, account-based innovation adds up to a significant competitive advantage for B2B companies. Henny Penny's collaboration with McDonald's resulted in a breakthrough product with a life of 8 to 12 years that pays back its cost in cooking-oil savings in less than 18 months. Accordingly, the company's LOV fryers command a premium position in the marketplace.

HCL, the IT services outsourcer introduced earlier in the book, used collaborative innovation to create mobile applications for a major customer in the beverage industry that allow its drivers and salespeople to access real-time inventory and product information, as well as provide management with a means of communicating instantly with its far-flung field operations. This technology enabled the company to change prices on the fly, run promotions in a timelier manner, and develop other real-time applications that improved the customer's bottom line by enhancing efficiency and effectiveness. Furthermore, this and other mobile applications were then vetted through the ECAC and subsequently rolled out to HCL's retail vertical market with great success.

ABI Engagement Map

Exhibit 6-4 illustrates the typical structure of an ABI program, its participants, and the principal connection points between B2B companies (the host companies) and their customers.

Exhibit 6-4: ABI Program Engagement Map

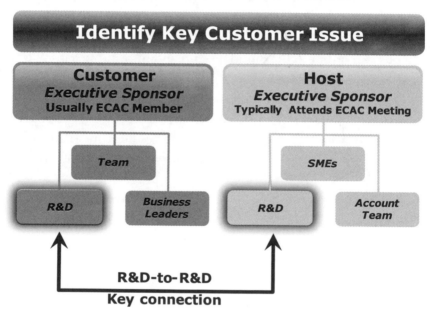

Source: Geehan Group

The leadership role in ABI is most important. The executive sponsor from the host company must understand the customer's environment and organizational goals, as well as the key issues and challenges. This understanding provides the host sponsor with the information needed to populate the ABI initiative with the right people from within his company (typically drawn from R&D, engineering, the account team, and other subject matter experts) and prepare them to work with the customer's team. Further, the host sponsor should not be part of the customer account team or have a direct financial stake (commission or bonus) that is directly tied to the customer. This restriction helps keep ABI focused on the higher goal of building a mutually beneficial future with the customer, instead of devolving the interaction into a sales transaction.

The key point in both examples: collaborative innovation delivers mutual value. In the B2B world, all great destinations are reached through your customer's world.

The Hierarchy of B2B Customer Engagement

Conventional wisdom says every customer deserves the same amount of attention and investment, but that has never been true in the B2B world. Not every B2B customer is a viable candidate for the levels of executive effort and interaction required to produce successful ABI initiatives and elevate a company's relationship with a customer to the level of business partner. For one thing, it is impractical for the senior executives of a B2B company to engage with each and every customer at this level of intensity; there simply isn't time. For another, not every customer account generates enough sales volume to produce an ROI that justifies an investment in ABI.

To make the most effective use of executive time and resources, B2B companies should segment their customers into a hierarchy defined by revenue, margin contribution, and strategic value (see Exhibit 6-5).

Exhibit 6-5: The Hierarchy Pyramid of Customer Engagement

Source: Geehan Group

In the typical B2B company, most customers will be located at the bottom of the engagement hierarchy pyramid. These are customers big enough to justify an account manager who is charged with retaining and growing the account. The second level of hierarchy should include customers who are large enough to justify participation in a major account program and the time of a small account team, usually including a sales manager and support personnel. For these two segments, the objective is to build the accounts and, if and when justified, try to move them farther along the Relationship Continuum.

The third level includes customers that are large enough to warrant inclusion in the ECAC—as we've seen these are executive customers who represent the top 5 percent to 20 percent of a B2B company's customer base. They receive a good deal of attention in a collective sense, as outlined earlier.

Finally, at the peak of the hierarchy, there are those few B2B customers whose long-term strategic value justifies one-on-one attention from the senior management team and inclusion in ABI programs.

This is truly a small subset of customers, whose value to the B2B company justifies the effort required to serve as a business partner and seek full institutional interdependence. B2B companies can enjoy plenty of growth by working with non-ABI customers. The time devoted to customers at the top of the hierarchy is most likely to pay off with innovations that command premium pricing and margins, and entirely new revenue streams applicable to complete segments or industries.

At Oracle, ABI is the ultimate program in the firm's customer engagement suite. It exists solely to build relationships at the highest level. "Partnership on paper means nothing," says executive vice president Keith Block. "You really have to commit and engage on both sides to be successful." Block believes Oracle's ABI initiative has been successful because the company has kept it completely separate from its sales initiatives. Because of this, Oracle's customers believe the company is entirely sincere in its desire to build collaborative, long-term relationships with them.

A Relationship Roadmap

So how does a B2B company move customers farther along the Relationship Continuum? To answer this question, we have developed a Relationship Roadmap (Exhibit 6-6) to outline the types of conversations necessary to move yourself up the B2B Relationship Continuum. The grid is constructed to demonstrate at each point of the continuum the following factors:

- The *Offerings* relevant at each level. For instance, if your offering needs customization for each customer, you must position yourself at least at the Problem Solver level, if not higher. Likewise for services such as facilities management as I discussed earlier. On the other hand, if you are selling a fairly standard product, and have no aspirations to broaden your portfolio or move into services, you do not need to invest the time and resources necessary to position yourself at the highest levels. Getting yourself to the Problem Solver level will give you a significant boost in margin.

- Once you have determined your type of *Offering*, you can look to see what type of Relationship is required and how to build it.

- Consider the *Customer Contact* with whom your company must have a relationship.

- Determine the *Relationship Owner* within your own organization.

- Focus on the *Types of Conversations* or discussion that must take place between the Customer Contact and your company's Relationship Owner.

- The *RFP (Request for Proposal) Interaction* is necessary to secure new and additional business. This column can also be used as an indicator of where you actually lie on the continuum today (much like the phone call test). If you think your customers see you as Trusted Advisor but you are only responding to pre-written RFPs, chances are you are a Reliable Supplier at best.

Exhibit 6-6: The B2B Relationship Roadmap

	Commodity Supplier	Reliable Supplier	Problem Solver	Trusted Advisor	Business Partner
Offerings	Off the shelf	Off the shelf	Off the shelf	Mass customized	Highly customized
Customer Contact	Procurement	Some low-level managers	Mid-level managers	Vice presidents or higher	Senior executives/ C-suite
Relationship Owner	Telesales/ website	Sales rep	Sales rep and SME	Account team (AM, consultant, specialist)	Non-sales executive
Types of Conversations	Product/price	Needs based	Business conversations	Business conversation, some strategy	Collaborative strategy/account-based innovation
RFP Interaction	Respond to all RFPs	Respond to qualified RFPs	Help write qualified RFPs	Oversees entire RFP process	Not applicable

Source: Geehan Group

The Relationship Roadmap shows that building Interdependency must occur at the decision-maker level, which is your customer executive. It also provides clarity on where you are today, where you need to invest in relationships, and who to engage both inside and outside your organization to move to your desired point on the continuum.

Far too often, B2B companies treat relationship building with their best customers as an exercise in entertainment. While taking customers to sporting events and restaurants is fine, these are pale substitutes for collaborative innovation, in which a company and one of its top customers creates something that neither party could have achieved on its own. This is the only sound foundation for an interdependent partnership based on trust, equality, accomplishment, mutual respect, and pride that delivers mutual value.

CHAPTER 7

GROW

LEVERAGING CUSTOMER ADVOCATES

*I*n 2007, Intesource was in a downward spiral. Growth had stalled and the company was losing money at an accelerating rate. This was all happening in an industry experiencing solid growth. The Board of Directors was faced with a simple choice: either close the company doors or give Tom Webster, then the procurement solution provider's chief marketing officer (CMO), a chance to get Intesource back on a profitable growth course. They chose Webster.

When Webster took over as CEO, Intesource's relationships with its best customers were on the rocks. They liked the company's offerings, but the prior CEO's abrasive style had alienated many of them. The new CEO faced four major challenges:

- Reduce operating costs

- Repair relationships with customers

- Get the company's employees re-energized

- Deliver a plan for profitable growth

Six customers that delivered 80 percent of Intesource's annual revenues were key to the company's survival. Losing any of them would have killed the company. But Webster knew if they could be retained and enlisted as committed supporters, they could also give Intesource a new lease on life. Accordingly, the company's leadership team immediately implemented a plan to retain these top accounts, elevate its relationships with them (which up to this point were anchored at user levels), and tap their executive customers for the market insight Intesource would need to turn its fortunes around.

"What drove our change, and ultimately our success, was getting our leaders in the same room with the real decision makers in our top customers," recalls Webster. "Once this happened, everything began to change quickly, including our clarity and alignment, as well as our direction and confidence to develop a bold strategic plan." Intesource's key customers became a part of its team and participated in its planning process. The company also pursued collaborative innovation with these customers on a one-on-one basis. But to achieve the aggressive growth goals needed to secure Intesource's future survival, the company also needed to acquire new customers at twice the industry rate.

Intesource needed to tap into the power of customer advocacy, which is the goal of the fourth and final step in *The B2B Executive Playbook*. The most efficient and effective means of winning new accounts and generating new revenue is to utilize the greatest resource in the company sales arsenal—existing customers. Executive customers in existing accounts know your offerings well. They possess the business knowledge, perspective, and credibility needed to convince decision makers at prospective customers (their peers) to buy. And if they can be effectively engaged, they can be highly motivated advocates in the marketplace.

Step 4 in *The B2B Executive Playbook* prescribes leveraging the relationships built through the first three steps to put the final knee in the B2B growth curve. It is aimed at developing executive customer advocacy that can:

- Drive new customer acquisition while reducing acquisition costs

- Grow the volume and margins in existing accounts

- Accelerate the sales cycle and raise close rates

The Power of Advocacy

The focus of the fourth and final step of *The B2B Executive Playbook* is creating SPPG by capitalizing on the planning and development activities undertaken in the early steps, and leveraging the trusted relationships built with executive customers. Almost invariably, by this point in the *Playbook*, a customer bond has been formed that is far stronger than the typical supplier-customer relationship. This bond is characterized by transparency, mutual loyalty, passion, and a true emotional stake in each other's welfare. Both B2B and the customer company are motivated to help each other succeed: each is an advocate of the other.

Advocacy is a powerful word. An advocate is someone who speaks or writes in favor of, supports or urges publicly for a cause. Advocates are typically proactive in their support; they look for opportunities to intercede on behalf of their causes.

Imagine the powerful effect of executive customers acting as advocates on behalf of your company. A business unit of a multibillion-dollar software company experienced firsthand this power several years ago, after one of its largest customers announced it was pulling all of its business because it believed that unit's billing software was causing errors adversely affecting the customer's relationships with its customers.

Leaders of the business unit were certain the software was not the culprit, but the customer would not give them a chance to plead their case. In desperation, they reached out to an ECAC that had been formed in another business unit. An ECAC member knew a senior executive at the defecting customer company, and secured an audience for the leaders of the business unit, who were then able to track the problem, prove that their software was not causing it, and save the account. Had that ECAC member not interceded, the company would have lost a large chunk of revenue, and its reputation would have suffered a major hit. Instead, the customer was so impressed that another customer was willing to be a personal advocate for the business unit, it renewed and expanded the relationship.

Leverage Top Customers to Acquire New Business and Expand Current Accounts

B2B companies don't have to be in dire straits to enlist the services of advocates. Executive customer advocates can and should be part of the extended B2B sales and marketing team. There are three venues in which executive customers shine as advocates:

- ***Decision-Maker Summits:*** Invitation-only events hosted by a B2B company to discuss issues, challenges, and aspirations important to decision makers within customer, prospect, and target accounts.

- ***Public Events:*** Events sponsored by third parties that are typically aimed at specific industries, functional specialties, or geographic areas.

- ***Reference Programs:*** Focused, facilitated interactions and discussions between existing customers and prospective buyers designed to raise close rates.

Decision-Maker Summits

Decision-maker summits go by a variety of names, such as round-tables and forums, but their basic ingredients and the expected results are always similar. In order to drive sales, a B2B company gathers its best customers to share their experience working with the company with target and prospective customers.

Summits usually feature customer advocates discussing key aspects of their relationship with the host company, including subjects such as the business value that the host has delivered and case studies of product and service success. Typically, these stories illuminate the host company's innovation, and support capabilities, as well as pertinent information regarding its culture, accessibility, and flexibility. There is no more powerful and credible punch than having top customers explain to targets and prospects what it is like to work with your company.

Exhibit 7-1: Executive Summits can be large or small gatherings, and typically include a keynote speaker, panel discussions, and/or breakout table discussions.

Nearly any size B2B company can host a decision-maker summit; they are within the financial means of even the leanest companies. And the payback in terms of driving awareness, positioning the company, building trusted relationships, and boosting sales is substantial. When done correctly, summits deliver benefits for everyone who attends and transform target companies into prospects and prospects into customers (see Exhibit 7-2).

Exhibit 7-2: The Benefits of Decision-Maker Summits

Host	Customers	Prospects
• Accelerate sales process	• Professional networking	• Professional networking
• Increase close rates	• Thought leadership opportunity	• Access to supplier executives
• Relationship building	• Validation of supplier	• Increased confidence in supplier
• Gain industry knowledge	• Access to host executives	• Peer exchange
• Leverage executive's time	• Peer exchange	• Best practices
	• Best practices	• Lessons learned
	• Lessons learned	

Source: Geehan Group

After Springer Science+Business Media developed strong ties with members of its ECACs, it began inviting them and others in the members' companies to present and participate in panel discussions at summits. The customers were encouraged to speak openly about challenges and obstacles they had faced, how they had overcome them, and the results of their interactions with Springer. "Having our best customers become advocates is a natural iteration for us, and the financial results have been incredible," says Syed Hasan.

Because decision-maker summits are designed around peer-to-peer interaction, they are six times more credible to potential customers than hearing the same information from a salesperson—and they are twice as credible than hearing the same information from a third party, such as an analyst or research firm. In fact, there is no more credible information source than a customer who has purchased and used a B2B company's offerings. Nothing compares to the depth and dimension of a firsthand story told by a customer in terms of building confidence among decision makers in prospective customer companies, especially just prior to signing a deal with a new supplier.

This confidence on the part of prospective customers translates directly into increased customer spending, an accelerated sales cycle, and higher close rates. Exhibit 7-3 summarizes the sales gains that 36 B2B companies recorded after holding one or more decision-maker summits.

Exhibit 7-3: ROI on Decision-Maker Summits

	Increased Spend	Sales Cycle Reduction	Close Rates w/Attendees
Current Customers	↑ 10-30%	↓ 10-30%	↑ 10-50%
Prospects		↓ 15-60%	↑ 30-300%

Source: Geehan Group Research

To date, Intesource has hosted four summits with top customers and sales prospects who repeatedly report it is the best educational event they attend during the year. More than 60 executives from more than 40 current and prospect accounts attended the fourth summit. Each summit begins with a welcome and brief 20-minute update on the company by CEO Tom Webster. Over two days, executive customers led the entire program, including every presentation, case study, panel, and work session.

With so many customers gathered together, most B2B companies would feel compelled to market and sell. But at Intesource, a commitment to customer inclusion in every aspect of the business is a cultural trait. As a result, the company resisted the temptation to sell and lived up to the promise with which Webster opened the summit: "This is your meeting and we're merely the facilitators."

There was no need for Intesource to do more: every presenter specifically mentioned that the company was instrumental to his or her success. And every presenter came well prepared and took pride in acting as an educator. Time and again, during breaks, attendees were saying things like, "I didn't know Intesource could do…" or "I need to learn how I can do that for our company." These are the kinds of comments that translate into growth opportunities.

Existing customers find summits as valuable as prospective customers. One of Intesource's customers announced in the last session that he'd been doing business with the company for more than seven years and had been to all four summits. "I have a whole list of new ideas I'm taking back to my company," he said. These ideas are sure to provide opportunities for Intesource to grow its business in an existing account.

> **"Listening and talking to my peers about how they addressed the challenges we all face and how Intesource played a role in their success was really eye-opening for me. And I appreciated the fact that the host didn't tout its products."**
>
> —An executive from a prospective customer
> company at an Intesource Summit

Intesource's summits not only generate a positive buzz in the market, they come with an ROI. After the fourth, Intesource recorded gains in deal flow, deal size, and new customer acquisition. "By having our customers talk about our solutions, it was exponentially more credible than us selling," says Tom Webster. "It was so real in content and a huge deal flow accelerator." The numbers back him up: sales prospects who attended had a close rate 300 percent higher than those who didn't. And time-to-close among this group was nearly cut in half, creating a significant boost to Intesource's cash flow. Decision-maker summits gave Intesource an ideal vehicle to meet its aggressive growth goals.

For Brad Cates, president of Standard Register's $246 million heath-care business unit, the goal was to reposition the business and accelerate awareness of the innovation and higher-value offerings they were bringing to market. They accomplished this by highlighting a major issue within health care (patient safety) and brought together the industry's thought leaders along with Standard Register's top customers and prospects. Cates shares, "Our business has evolved significantly in just the last few years. Our summit gave us an opportunity to reposition our organization with today's and tomorrow's market in a very credible and accelerated way."

Global executive program leader Gowrishankar Vembu at HCL shares, "Every 18 months we bring more than 800 clients, prospects, and industry thought leaders from around the world together. And the impact and credibility gained pays off in the both short-term and long-term."

Public Events

Public events sponsored by third parties are useful venues for getting face-to-face with prospects and seeking new sales opportunities. These events include industry and association conventions, and functional and professional gatherings. But it is always difficult for a B2B company to differentiate itself from the other sellers attending.

A good solution to this problem is to invite one or more of your executive customers to attend the event with you and share, either in a presentation or workshop, how you worked together to create value. As with decision-maker summits, potential customers in the audience who are facing similar challenges find these stories highly credible. As a result, they qualify themselves as sales candidates and contact you for follow-up conversations, filling your company's sales pipeline with high-conversion leads.

Public events are especially effective when B2B companies are seeking to maintain market awareness and/or leadership in high-growth or fast-changing conditions or are expanding into new geographical markets. They are also highly effective venues for repositioning when expanding a solution portfolio and launching new offerings in existing or new markets.

Repositioning is often challenging for B2B companies. When a company makes its mark doing something very well, the market begins to see the company in those terms. When the company seeks to expand its portfolio beyond those things, it must change limiting perceptions in order to gain acceptance. Often B2B companies invest huge amounts of money in the creation of marketing and branding campaigns to accomplish this feat. However, enlisting executive customers to present at public events is a much more cost-effective and credible means of achieving the same goal.

Crown Partners discovered this when one of its executive customers, a thought leader in his discipline, presented at an industry event. This well-respected executive not only helped accelerate Crown's sales cycle, he also helped the company reposition itself at higher levels with its customer base. "The impact was far greater than if someone from our company had been the speaker," recalls CEO Hearn.

Springer Science+Business Media used executive customers and public events to raise market awareness regarding changes in its business model that offer greater flexibility. The company asked early adopters of the options offered by the new model to share their stories.

Wells Fargo used this strategy to reinforce its position in the commercial banking market in the wake of the mortgage crisis in 2008 and its acquisition of Wachovia, which brought with it new services and a major geographic expansion. The bank's goal was to make the market aware of its new capabilities, while instilling confidence in current customers and prospective customers regarding its financial condition. "Having key commercial customers talk about the enhanced experience the merger brought was much more believable than any message we could have communicated ourselves," says senior vice president Jeff Tinker.

Reference Programs

Customer loyalty expert Fred Reichheld says the most important metric in any company is its "net promoter" score. This score measures the answers to what he calls the "ultimate" question: "How likely is it that you would recommend us to a friend or colleague?"

Reference programs with executive customers are a systematic method for maximizing the willingness and desire of customers to answer this question with a resounding "Highly likely!" The benefits of credible customer references showcasing a B2B company's value are well documented. Unfortunately, most B2B companies look for a high *quantity* of references alone. This usually results in user-level references because they are much easier to obtain, and are greater in number. Executive customers, on the other hand, are more compelled by references from their peers. The game changer in credibility and effectiveness with this audience is having a number of executive customers willing to advocate on your behalf in the form of a referral or reference.

Our findings indicate reference programs can accelerate the sales process by 20 to 60 percent and raise closing rates by 30 to 150 percent. According to Vicki Cooney, VP of marketing at $78 billion Pennsylvania-based AmerisourceBergen, "Our reference program has made a tangible difference in driving deal flow and ultimately closing deals. The credibility of a peer recommendation is unmatched."

Managing reference data, materials, and contacts presents a challenge for most companies as the gathering and use of recommendations is typically left to individual salespeople on a fairly ad hoc basis. Instead, what is needed for this valuable source of sales generation is a formal reference program that ensures a B2B company takes full advantage of executive customer recommendations.

Leading reference management solutions provider Point of Reference CEO David Sroka believes that, "Having a systematic approach is vital to yielding sustainable success." Sroka recommends a world-class reference program to:

- Establish an organizational database that identifies which executive customers are willing to serve as a reference, and houses their participation preferences.

- Ensure executive customers' willingness to participate is not abused or overused.

- Enable companies to organize and match customer references to sales prospects by company size, industry, internal environment, solution interests and configuration, or deal structure.

Customers can provide references in many ways: speaking to prospects in person or on the phone; participating in video testimonials; authoring case studies, articles, and newsletters; or by providing quotes for publication in marketing collateral, websites, blogs, and press releases (see Exhibit 7-4).

Exhibit 7-4: Customer Reference Approaches

Approach	Purpose	Setting	Sample Application
Speaking on behalf of host company	• Build awareness • Increase credibility • Generate leads • Overcome buying obstacles for prospects	• At a company hosted event • At an industry gathering or conference • Webinar	Issue-driven case study or best practice/ lessons learned presentation
Articles/ white papers	• To educate executive/decision maker prospects • Validation by showing tangible business value (ROI, etc.)	• For early-stage responses • Business-level content	Issue-driven case study or best practice/lessons learned article *(keep to under 2 pages or 1,000 words)*
Video	• To highlight specific issue/area of concern • Prospect evaluation	• For early stages of buying process	Case study broken down into 45- to 90-second sound bites on specific topics/issues
Written quotes	• Customers sharing experiences and/ or specific, credible proof points • CONFIRMATION	• Early or explorative part of sales process	Accolades on company to include on all sales collateral, website, proposals, etc. *(keep to 1–2 sentences)*
Peer-to-peer interaction	• Decision maker (customer) to decision maker (prospect) conversation about aspects of working with supplier (culture, style, etc.)	• Phone call between existing customer and prospect (supplier not on phone)	
Prospect site visit	• Influencer and users visit current customer who has product/system installed to see it in person		
Press release	• Customers sharing experiences and/ or specific credible proof points • Validation of great partnership	• Announce a renewed contract with quote from decision maker of customer sharing their commitment to key supplier with reasoning and/or proof of success	

Source: Geehan Group

Activating the Fourth Step—Growth

Over decades, LexisNexis built an incredible brand around legal research, and then started bringing some additional solutions to the legal market. Customers who purchased the new solutions loved them, but the problem was that not enough organizations were buying them. It was difficult to get LexisNexis customers to think beyond the core longstanding offering of online legal research. For one particular solution, there were many prospects that were simply stalled in the buying process.

One of the new solutions was different. All prospects identified as potential purchasers were already purchasers of the core LexisNexis research, so they liked and trusted the company. This new innovation, however, was a stretch with regard to the decision maker's perception of where LexisNexis stood on the B2B Relationship Continuum. Most saw LexisNexis as a Reliable Supplier, not a company who brought to market innovative products commanding a premium.

This struggle ended when LexisNexis enlisted early-adopter decision makers of the new solution to share stories and experiences with peer groups in a series of regional summits across the U.S. Results were immediate and measurable. In the following quarter, the number of closed deals for the new solution quadrupled and the sales cycle was reduced by more than 50 percent (from nine months to four months). LexisNexis's customers helped each other to understand the value of the new solution in a credible and compelling way.

The key to activating Step 4 of *The B2B Executive Playbook* is to enlist executive customers to create a safe, candid, and relevant dialogue about your solutions with their peers in the marketplace. The result isn't a sanitized marketing presentation. Your customers may mention weaknesses in the solution or problems they encountered in implementing it. In fact, the story they tell may not even be about the solution per se; it might be about the successful change effort their companies undertook or the new value they can now deliver to their customers. That's fine. These qualities make a story believable, and everyone who hears them knows why your company is providing the opportunity to hear them.

When we describe Step 4 to the leaders of B2B companies, the most common response is: "Why would all these busy executives come to a summit we run? We are just one among many vendors of theirs." Like most companies, Crown Partners, HCL, LexisNexis, Intesource, Wells Fargo, and Springer had similar concerns. And yet, all of them had tremendous success in securing commitment and engagement from executive customers. In the case of LexisNexis, some of these executives enjoyed participating in summits in their regions so much they asked to speak at summits in other regions.

The secret is preparing a sound foundation and strong relationships with executive customers in the first three steps of the *Playbook*, which LexisNexis had done very effectively. If the right seeds are planted and the right approach is taken, executive customers will not only make time to participate, they will drive your sales growth.

Today, Springer frequently uses its executive customers as advocates and references. And the company has an extensive database of customers who have volunteered for:

- Participating in a case study

- Siiting on a panel

- Providing quotes and recommendations

- Contributing Springer newsletter articles

- Co-authoring a white paper .

- Speaking at events and summits

- Talking directly with Springer prospects

Oracle's executive customers also play an integral role in the company's sales process as loyal advocates of its products and services. "It's magic," declares chief customer officer Jeb Dasteel. "If you look at our most loyal customers and best references, they tend to be those who are most engaged. And the way they get actively engaged is through the structured customer programs we've built."

"This is a way of creating relationships that has nothing to do with a particular transaction," he continues. "It's to the point that these customers may not be completely thrilled with every aspect of the offering they recently implemented, but they are still willing to be strong references for us because of the relationship we've built. They are willing to put their reputations on the line to endorse us, and we take that trust very seriously."

CHAPTER 8

IMPLEMENTING THE PLAYBOOK

*I*mplementing all four steps of *The B2B Executive Playbook* usually takes 18 to 24 months, although we have seen companies accomplish this in as few as 9 to 12 months. The strategic payoff, which comes in the form of internal and market alignment and more effective planning, typically becomes apparent in 6 to 9 months. The financial payoff—enhanced account growth and retention, more successful development efforts, improved sales and marketing ROI, and increased margins—begins around the 9 to 12 month mark. Finally, within 12 to 24 months, companies begin to realize the ultimate payoff from their executive customer programs: sustainable, predictable, and profitable growth.

In larger companies (those more than $2 billon), executive customer programs are typically organized in business units rather than at the corporate level. There are two reasons why this is usually the more practical choice. First, crossing too many internal boundaries can add complexity to program management, especially as more and more businesses become involved. Second, the ability to focus programs on one line of business ensures they will be consistently relevant to the executive customers participating. Running separate initiatives makes more sense when the issues and topics important to respective customer decision makers are unique to each business unit or product portfolio.

Many large B2B companies apply the *Playbook* independently for each business unit. Cisco Systems, Inc., for example, has dozens of executive customer programs due to the diverse markets and geographies it serves. Springer Science +Business Media has separate initiatives for different geographic regions (North America, South America, Asia, Europe, and the Middle East) and markets (academic and corporate).

Business unit ownership also works best in companies serving both B2B and B2C markets, such as Wells Fargo and Dell. As we've seen, the issues and needs are so different in each realm that mixing B2B and B2C audiences or their respective playbooks is simply not feasible.

No matter how large the company, there is no need to begin an executive customer initiative with a vast commitment and budget. Oracle has one of the most complex and effective customer executive program structures in the B2B world, but the company started small with a modest vision and one initiative. It established metrics and ROI milestones to keep the momentum going and ensure that internal sponsors embraced and applied the *Playbook*. And it grew its programs from there.

Playbook Roles and Responsibilities

Like most strategic-level initiatives, the success of executive customer programs and the speed of their implementation and development are highly dependent on the involvement of the senior leadership team in the company or business unit. This team usually includes the P&L owner (CEO, president, or business unit head), as well as heads of functions, including strategy, finance, R&D, marketing, sales, and service. These executives split among themselves program management and responsibility for program success (see Exhibit 8-1).

Exhibit 8-1: B2B Playbook Implementation—Executive Roles

B2B Playbook Executive Role	B2B Playbook Responsibilities
Executive Sponsor *P&L Owner: President, CEO, or BU Head*	• Provides the accountability and authority within organization needed to muster executive presence and support for the initiative • Ensures insights and ideas identified during programs are assessed and acted upon within the organization • Casts a "wide enough" net of responsibility to establish and oversee all *Playbook* programs • Engaged as needed to drive and validate planning, priority setting, and resource allocation
Champion *Typically a Marketing or Strategy leader*	• Manages the overall sequencing and integration of the *Playbook* • Liaison to entire leadership team and company. Responsible for engaging the leadership team in the initiative as appropriate based on its goals • Responsible for overall execution, but not involved in day-to-day activities
Project Manager *Typically from Marketing*	• Manages the day-to-day activities and details surrounding the entire initiative • Works with all stakeholders to integrate the *Playbook* • Leads communications to company
Key Stakeholders *Functional heads: Sales, Marketing, Strategy, Development, Finance, Service*	• Engaged early in the program to set the stage for both team and market alignment • Attends Council meetings and serves as lead sponsors in one-to-one account activities

Source: Geehan Group

To the President or CEO (P&L owner of business unit or company)

As the head of a B2B company or business unit, and its most influential employee, you should be the sponsor of the executive customer initiative. Whether your organization chooses to implement some or all of *The B2B Executive Playbook*, it is important to understand these programs can bolster the performance of the entire organization and, thus, should involve many functional areas. Too often, B2B companies relegate executive customer programs to marketing and sales functions and miss the benefits for strategic planning and R&D. If you decide to invest in executive customer programs, please get your money's worth!

Once *Playbook* implementation begins, it's critical that the entire senior leadership team is involved in ECAC meetings. Internal alignment that streamlines strategic planning depends on face-to-face interaction with top customers. Your team needs to hear the collective voice of its executive customers so everyone has the same reference points. This raises the level of strategy discussions and ensures they are properly market-focused (versus an internal focus, which inevitably becomes more tactical and numbers-driven).

When Standard Register, a document and information management solution provider with $668 million in annual revenues, undertook its executive customer initiative, CEO Joe Morgan immediately realized he needed to own the *Playbook*. He also charged and empowered his business unit leaders to drive the *Playbook* within their respective organizations and markets. It was the only way to ensure the company was asking the right questions and gaining the clarity and confidence needed to make bold decisions in a business environment where customer demands and new technology presented almost continuous transformation. "When I became CEO, status quo was not an option," explained Morgan. "I recognized there were certain areas I could not abdicate—and this was absolutely one of them."

> *"Having a P&L leader sponsoring executive customer programs results in transformational rather than incremental impact. It's the most effective and powerful way we have to drive market and internal alignment, and ultimately, our long-term success."*

-- Scott Collins, Vice President
and head of the Law School business unit, LexisNexis.

To Strategy Leaders

Many B2B companies use SWOT analysis as a foundational tool in the strategic planning processes, but the input and feedback of a market collective should be applied no matter what planning approach your company uses. For instance, Michael Porter's Five Forces analysis is still a fine tool for planning, but the force of "buyer power" would be weighted based on the company's concentration of top customers.

The strategist's approach is often limited by the confines imposed by the current reality. But strategy leaders must also include the mid- and long-term (3 to 5 years) views in the planning process. To incorporate this perspective, conversations with market collectives should be designed to ensure discussions do not become too product-centric or overly focused on short-term demands. Challenge the internal leadership team to talk about the future, and ask ECAC members to describe operational and business aspirations of their companies.

In terms of SWOT analyses, focus strategic conversations with the market collective on opportunities and threats while simply testing and validating their perceptions of the strengths and weaknesses. Bring leaders of the M&A function to ECAC meetings, if your company is considering making acquisitions. The input of ECAC members is often extremely helpful when evaluating potential target firms. "The guidelines in the *Playbook* have helped us achieve our aggressive growth goals of more than 50 percent per year," explains HCL's ISD strategy leader Anubhav Saxena. "Incorporating the Market-Aligned Planning process enables us to vet the major ideas, which gives our team the confidence to make bold strategic decisions, including identifying potential investments and acquisitions."

To Sales Leaders

Executive customer programs are an essential support and driver of the sales goals of a B2B company. As sales leader, you can help identify executive customers and encourage them to interact directly with your company's leadership team. This direct line of communication should provide you and your sales team with peace of mind: you will know that the priorities and investments your company makes will better meet market needs . . . and that means more sales.

Indeed, ECAC members are an invaluable sales asset. First, they share their specific needs. Second, they share how they want to buy, helping you redesign and refine your sales process and salesforce training. Third, they become internal sponsors within their firms, driving enhanced sales opportunities. Finally, they become wonderful advocates and references, helping you secure new customers and business.

Your sales team is the biggest functional beneficiary of the *Playbook* because executive customers help it exceed quotas and minimize margin erosion. According to LexisNexis SVP of Sales, Keith Hawk, "Members of the sales organization were hesitant to support the *Playbook* initiatives, but once they recognized the value of the programs, they fully endorsed them. It's important to have the patience and tenacity to get over that hump."

To Financial Leaders

As your company's chief financial officer, your participation in executive customer programs is essential to ensure the company's resources are being allocated in ways that are aligned with the right markets and to specific needs in each market. Further, if you serve as an executive sponsor for a key account, the experience will heighten your understanding of the customer's world and external conditions that determine sales and development success, and enhance your internal effectiveness.

You should create a scorecard for the company's executive customer programs' ROI and ensure they meet company investment and parameter needs, as well as benchmarks for programs of this type. As we've shown, all executive customer programs should deliver a healthy ROI.

"Our executive customer initiatives, built around our important customers at the decision-maker levels, have proven to be the most effective way to positively impact top and bottom line results," states Jeff Garrity, CFO of NCR's Services Division. "Their ROI is undeniable across the organization, but the CFO needs to be engaged to properly track and support them."

As executive customer initiatives begin to suggest new directions for investment, your guidance is particularly important.

Key questions to ask as new marketing campaigns are proposed include:

- What is the balance of spend among users, influencers, and decision makers?

- What is the balance of spend between account retention and new account acquisition?

Key questions to ask of new R&D projects include:

- What is the business value to the customer decision maker in this project?

- How will customer decision makers measure the value/return of this purchase?

- What problem is the project trying to solve for the market?

The answers to questions like these provide valuable insight into how to maximize returns on your discretionary investments.

To Marketing Leaders

Traditionally, marketing has not played as significant a role in B2B companies as it does in B2C companies, but B2B marketing's time has come! B2B marketers are expanding from internal marketing activities (such as marketing communications and operations) to a much broader role which seeks to include strategic issues like profitable growth and widening margins. Gary Slack, President of Business Marketing Association (BMA), one of the largest B2B associations, calls this moving from "little m" to "big M" marketing. "B2B marketing leaders must get out of the silos," Slack says, "connecting, contributing and adding value to other parts of the business and directly impacting revenue and profits."

Management of executive customer programs provides a tremendous opportunity for marketing leaders to earn a seat at the table and raise their profiles in the B2B world. Through program management, marketing can help drive strategic planning, guide the innovation roadmap, and even identify acquisition targets. In addition, marketing leaders can become a catalyst for SPPG.

With its discretionary budgets and insight into customers and the marketplace, marketing is a natural liaison among the various go-to-market functions in a B2B company. The "big M" marketing leader can and should connect and lead cross-functional executive customer initiatives—solidifying marketing's relationship with sales and R&D, and becoming a valuable adjunct to the CEO or business unit head.

The broad, cross-functional application of executive customer programs requires all senior leadership members of B2B companies or business units to play important roles and have essential responsibilities. The degree to which they embrace and fulfill these roles and responsibilities will determine the return a B2B company earns on its executive customer initiatives and its success in creating SPPG.

CHAPTER 9

AVOIDING THE FOUR PITFALLS

*T*he *B2B Executive Playbook* describes four steps that can simplify strategic planning, focus product development and sales and marketing efforts, and, most importantly, create a clear path to market leadership. If implemented properly, it will also add sustainability and predictability to a B2B company's top and bottom lines.

As with any corporate initiative, however, success can be sidetracked if problematic modes of operating and behavior creep in. This chapter reviews four common pitfalls that prevent B2B firms from succeeding that my colleagues and I have witnessed over the years. Be aware of them, and act quickly if they surface in your company.

Pitfall #1: Inside-Only Thinking

The first pitfall is a mindset among the leadership team that goes something like this: "Hey, we're smart and we've been in this industry for many years. Let's brainstorm among ourselves and come up with the next great solution we can bring to market to change the game and win back our leadership position." The leadership teams of B2B companies do have deep stores of knowledge and creativity, but when they choose to go it alone, what they are really saying is, "We know better than our customers what they want and need." And this is a prescription for failure.

Far too often, the inside-only ideas and solutions that come out of these sessions are not created with current market conditions or even company resources, business models, and competencies in mind. In fact, they are usually based on legacy customer needs, current competitor offerings, or misguided ideas about a problem that may not even exist in the customer's mind. This insular approach significantly contributes to the 60-70 percent product failure rate that continues to plague companies.

Case: The leaders of a $1 billion company invested more than $100 million in developing a single solution they were convinced would revolutionize their market. They did this without asking a single customer to validate the idea. The result was a disaster. Virtually no customers wanted the solution because it couldn't be integrated with their existing operations, and the few who did buy, demanded to return it for a full refund, plus damages. The stock tumbled, the leadership team was fired, and the company was sold off at a major discount to a company one-fifth its size.

Bottom Line: Successful B2B companies avoid inside-only thinking. At Henny Penny, for example, all innovation and planning initiatives begin with the needs of customers and the market. "This is the backbone of our culture, strategic planning, and success," explains President Rob Connelly. "It has enabled us to hold on to and grow our biggest customers for decades, because our plans help them serve their customers more effectively."

With so many strategic and development alternatives to chose from, you must tap your top customers to prioritize, justify, and focus on those options that will deliver the most impact. Leveraging their industry knowledge through "outside-inside" thinking is the only way to secure market alignment and win over the long-term.

Pitfall #2: Limiting Input to End-Users

The second pitfall is triggered when B2B companies depend too heavily on customer input gathered from end users. This overdependence usually results in more of the same. Most companies are very good at establishing customer dialogue at this level. However, end user input is typically focused on product improvements aimed at maximizing the user experience. As Henry Ford is reputed to have said, "If I'd asked my customers what they wanted, they'd have said a faster horse."

The problem with endlessly adding features and functionality to products is that at some point it no longer adds business value for the customer. And if there is no added value, executive customers will not pay a premium for incremental improvements. Thus, more bells and whistles equal higher costs and lower margins.

"We were too focused on the users we interacted with and not on the business issues we were hired to solve," recalls Crown Partners' CEO Hearn. "We were talking to people at the wrong level. We got off track and began to marginalize our business and value."

Case: A $100 million manufacturer produces high-quality industrial tubing that is the Rolls Royce of its market. This tubing exceeds the current industry standard for tolerance by 50 percent; the product has never failed in the field. When we met with the company's leaders, they proudly informed us that they were working to raise the tubing's tolerance to 100 percent above the industry standard.

This excited customer engineers (end users of the tubing), who thought the additional tolerance would be "great to have." Unfortunately, no customer projects or plans required anywhere near this new tolerance level. Further, executive customers knew the proposed tubing far exceeded tolerance levels that had been successful for decades, and they saw no reason to pay a premium for it. It was a classic example of over-engineering in pursuit of a better user experience.

In the B2C world, where the consumer is the user and the decision maker, it works just fine. I'm thirsty. I buy and drink a Diet Coke. If I like it, I do it again and again. But in the B2B world, user satisfaction does not necessarily result in customer retention or increased sales.

> *"Once we understood the differences each customer level brought to the table for us, it opened us up to ideas and ways of doing business that we would have never considered. Now we know each level's value and how to engage them effectively."*

— Tim Thorsteinson, former President
Harris Corporation, Broadcast Communications Division

Bottom line: Ultimately, executive customers fund your company and decide with their dollars whether your strategy (in terms of offerings, pricing models, direction of industry, etc.) is successful. You should secure input from as many customer levels—purchasing agents, users, influencers, and decision makers—as your budget and resources allow, but always remember that it is the decision maker's input that matters most. So, start with your executive customers.

Pitfall #3: Following a Single Customer

It's a common story: A new CEO takes the reins and goes to visit the company's key customers to establish relationships, make sure promises are being met, say thanks, and offer access. On each of these visits, the CEO asks the CEO at the customer company, "What are your biggest issues?" and "What keeps you up at night?" Terrific questions.

But then things start to unravel. The CEO hears something at one account that strikes a chord. A BIG idea. He comes home and redirects the company's development teams, strategy, and resources, based on a single conversation.

Case: The CEO of a $10 billion manufacturing services company met with the president of his company's biggest customer. The president suggested a solution to a problem with which he said 20 other major players in his industry were also struggling. This convinced the CEO to invest more than $100 million in developing the solution. Two years later, no one, including the original customer, was willing to buy the solution. The B2B seller had rechanneled its key resources, lost credibility in the market, fallen behind its competitors, and ended up writing off the entire project.

Bottom line: The only way to secure market alignment is to enlist a market *collective* to validate direction and major development projects. Most B2B offerings need a market, not just one customer.

Pitfall #4: Chasing the Competition

Chasing your competitors is the fastest path to the bottom, with only two possible outcomes: First, there is a very strong possibility you are following a competitor that doesn't know where it's going—and you will follow them down. Second, there is the possibility the competitor is right—and you will finish in second place. Even if you do succeed in achieving sustainable, predictable, profitable growth in this way, you will only achieve it *after* your competitors. Stanford Graduate School of Business professor William Barnett calls this "Red Queen Competition"—you run faster and faster, but you never get ahead.

Bottom line: If you chase your competitors, they will always have the edge. Don't put your fate in your competitor's hands.

In the end, only one path to sustainable, predictable, profitable growth will yield industry leadership: a strategy grounded in the intersections between the needs of the market and a B2B company's business model and core competencies (see Exhibit 9-1).

Exhibit 9-1: The Source of Competitive Advantage

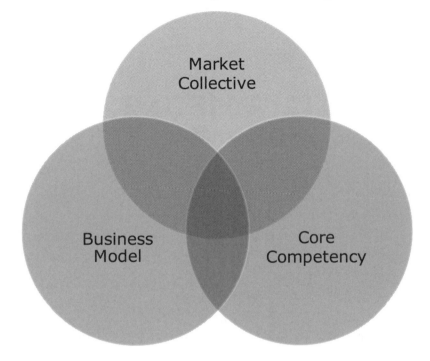

Executive customer-focused strategies and tactics in *The B2B Executive Playbook* enable B2B companies to avoid the four common pitfalls. But even with this *Playbook* as your guide, it will take constant vigilance and commitment to gain the full benefits of your executive customer programs.

LIGHT LIFTING, HIGH IMPACT

Executives' time and resources are among the most valuable assets in B2B companies. With leadership teams being pulled in so many directions, it has become more and more difficult for them to effectively manage and leverage their time. I wrote *The B2B Executive Playbook* based on best practices designed by firm to provide B2B leaders with a light-lifting, high-impact approach to running their businesses.

Implementing the four steps in the *Playbook* will not add more "stuff" to the already-overloaded executive agenda. Rather, it will significantly reduce the amount of time and effort currently devoted to wasteful activities, ineffective programs, and frustrating distractions. It gives B2B leadership teams the greatest gift of all: more quality time to think, plan, and execute. In addition to driving profitable growth and reducing costs, the *Playbook* helps your team:

1. Gain focus, clarity, confidence, and buy-in when setting the strategic direction of your company

2. Save valuable time and resources throughout your organization

3. Establish and increase leadership credibility internally and in the market

4. Create a purposeful customer-centric culture

Gain Strategic Focus, Clarity, Confidence, and Buy-in

The comment we hear most often from top leaders is the high-impact executive customers have on strategic planning. But don't just take our word for it—hear it from your peers.

"The approach set forth in the *Playbook* was an epiphany for me and my team," says Harris Morris, President of Harris Broadcast. "It helped us set our course, gave us much more focus, and enabled us to more boldly and confidently take calculated risks. The principles of the *Playbook* provided us with the confidence to kill products and programs that just weren't working."

The B2B Executive Playbook also proved instrumental in the turnaround at Intesource, especially when newly appointed CEO Tom Webster needed to get the company's leadership on board and quickly formulate a turnaround plan that set a new direction and allocated scarce resources. "This approach made gaining support, securing alignment, and generating excitement significantly easier with both my board, which funded the plan, and the employees, who executed it," says Webster.

Save Time and Resources

With focus and clarity, prioritization becomes much easier. The *Playbook* helps leadership teams recognize which programs and resources are helping achieve organizational goals, and which activities are less-than-effective investments of time and money. From killing products and services, whether already on the market or in development, to halting unproductive sales activities and marketing programs, the executive team will be much more aligned and will stop wasting time confusing activities with results.

"There have been countless times when we wanted to go down certain paths, due to competition, advice from consultants, extra cash, etc.," recalls Wells Fargo Commercial Group senior vice president Jeff

Tinker, "but the elements of this system kept us from wasting time and resources on activities, products, and services that wouldn't add value or would not support our strategy and priorities. This not only saved us significant time, but enhanced our bottom line."

Establish and Increase Leadership Credibility

Nothing can sink a company as fast as a senior team that does not believe in the company's leader or in his or her decisions. That's why leadership gurus Jim Kouzes and Barry Posner identified credibility as critical for any leader, and particularly for new leaders who have come from another part of the company or from another company or industry.

The B2B Executive Playbook enhances leadership credibility because it assures direct reports and boards that a leader's decisions are aligned to the market. When leaders are credible, they accomplish more and can motivate others to accomplish more.

Scott Collins discovered this dynamic when he was brought in from outside to rebuild LexisNexis's market share among law schools. "When I joined LexisNexis, my direct reports averaged a dozen years of experience in the industry and with LexisNexis. On top of that, most had attended law school themselves and were attorneys, experience I did not have," says Collins. "These key programs accelerated my ability to quickly gain credibility and trust among my team and with our most important customers. If I didn't have that, transforming this part of the business would have been impossible."

Recently appointed Harris Broadcast President Harris Morris had a similar experience. "The transition from vice president to president was much easier because I didn't have to set the direction or sell a direction to my team," he says. "With this approach, the direction had been set by the market. I simply needed to facilitate the process, which was a much easier task."

When Tom Webster was promoted from within Intesource to become CEO, his challenge was to gain credibility as the top leader among those who had previously been his peers. He accomplished this by letting the market do the talking. "My philosophy throughout my career is that the market will provide the direction, if you listen," says Webster. "The *Playbook* translates that philosophy into a tangible game plan for leadership teams, not by arm-twisting or making concessions that aren't truly in the best interest of the market or the organization."

Create a Purposeful Customer-centric Culture

Finally, the *Playbook* provides a tangible way to instill and maintain a strong customer focus and commitment in a corporate culture. Thomas Kurian, Oracle's executive vice president, is convinced that aligning strategy and development around customer business objectives is a core component of his company's success. And the *Playbook* has helped keep customers at the heart of Oracle's vision to deliver.

At Springer Science+Business Media, the entire leadership team, including the chairman, CEO, and regional leaders, supports customer input and engagement programs as the starting point of their strategy. "We are all directly and actively involved," says Syed Hasan. "The payoff is that the *Playbook* has helped drive our strategic transformation and fuel our growth, allowing us to soar past the competition."

I hope this book has convinced you that applying executive customer programs can help produce sustainable, predictable, profitable growth for your company and, as importantly, increase your leadership credibility, impact, and longevity. Thank you for taking this journey with me. I wish you every success as you seek to guide your company to the next level in the journey to market leadership.

MARKETING AND SOCIAL MEDIA

I have included a section about leveraging the marketing arm of an organization to create true value for the company, as well as a view of the rapidly changing and growing B2B social media (SM) world.

My observation is that leadership teams struggle to find consistent value, credibility, and tangible results from the activities coming out of the marketing organizations in B2B companies.

Concepts shared here have helped executives across the organization, especially the CEO, CFO, and the heads of Sales, R&D and Strategy, understand the business value marketing can bring to the table and the financial impact it can have. Additionally, they have brought clarity about how the B2B marketing organization can be more effective. In it, you will find information on budgeting, maximizing margin yield, branding, ROI, positioning, and how oftentimes activities get confused with results.

In this section a few concepts are repeated from the book. I did this to provide a single, common reference point for the leadership team regarding B2B marketing. It also provides greater continuity and is easier to follow by not referencing page numbers and graphics earlier in the book. I hope you'll agree.

On the social media front, everything is exploding. While I have some perspective on how and where social media is being applied in the B2B world, I thought you'd really appreciate having SM guru and best-selling author Paul Dunay share his observations, recommendations, and advice, since he has been completely focused on this and is the recognized leader. See page 165 for the complete interview with Paul.

LEVERAGING MARKETING TO DRIVE ORGANIZATIONAL VALUE

Gary Slack, president of one of the largest B2B associations, Business Marketing Association (BMA), believes marketers need to take a larger, more significant role in B2B organizations. This means moving from exclusively internal marketing activities (marketing communication and operation) to a much broader role that includes organizational issues like profitable growth and widening margins. He calls it "Little m and Big M marketing." Slack says, "Marketing leaders must get out of the silos, connecting, contributing, and adding value to other parts of the business and directly impacting revenue and profits."

The B2B Playbook provides marketing executives the opportunity to become Big M marketers, impact the entire organization, and connect and strategically lead cross-functional initiatives. Doing so solidifies the relationship between marketing and sales as well as finance, R&D, service, and strategy.

Now is a tremendous time for marketing to earn a "seat at the table" in a B2B business unit or company. Earlier in the book we highlighted how marketing can drive organizational planning as well as guide the innovation roadmap and identify acquisition targets.

In addition, marketing leaders can be catalysts for the entire organization and be viewed by the CEO as key drivers of sustainable, predictable, profitable growth (SPPG). This goal helps you reach the endgame: maximizing shareholder wealth.

Samir Bagga, U.S. vice president of marketing at $3 billion Indian-based IT services company HCL, explained that the *Playbook*'s framework has helped him plug into parts of the organization where marketing can really make a difference to the entire organization's success.

The Great Marketing Divide

One of the biggest differences between B2B and B2C is marketing. Many extremely successful marketing leaders in B2C have a difficult time making the much-needed adjustments to be successful.

In Chapter 2, I referenced Michael Jordan's struggles to make the leap from the most elite basketball player of all time to playing on a minor league baseball team. I've witnessed dozens of successful B2C marketing executives who met the same fate as Jordan did when they crossed over from a B2C to a B2B organization.

Often, I run into high-profile marketing executives much like the one I worked with from a major soft drink company. He amassed all kinds of accolades and had great success at his former company as a brand leader of its flagship product. His honors included national advertising and marketing awards as well as several industry awards. The financials were incredible too…market share gains and profitable growth. He moved to a B2B company and applied the same B2C formula that made him a huge success at his old company.

His new company had 10,000 customers, but their top 50 customers comprised 50 percent of the company's revenue. The top 200 were around 75 percent of the revenue of this $4 billion company. He didn't fully understand the impact of this concentration of revenue and violated nearly every B2B success principle outlined in this book. Most of what he did was in the name of branding, (new look, logo, tagline, positioning, etc.). He committed millions to what made him wildly successful at his B2C company.

The results were brutal: sales went down, market share slid, margins tumbled, and because he also oversaw and shifted R&D dollars to marketing, their product started to become commoditized because they weren't reinvesting like the competition. In addition, many of their top customers were leaving them, signing exclusive long-term deals with the competition—never to return. The only thing that collapsed more than the financial results was company morale.

According to Spencer Stuart, a global executive search firm, the CMO position has been the shortest-tenured C-level position for the last seven consecutive years—roughly 20 months. The individual mentioned above lasted three years. He has been gone for about three years now, and this company still hasn't fully recovered from the damage the B2C applications caused to this great B2B company. Like Michael Jordan, he failed to successfully switch sports.

Critical Success Factors of B2B Marketing

Four critical success factors will elevate the role of marketing and support the success of the *Playbook*. The first of these success factors relates directly to the issues relevant to the CEO, CFO, and marketing leader. The second critical success factor provides insight for the CFO, explaining how ROI can be increased. The final two success factors discuss the importance of obtaining relevant input and general marketing best practices.

In addition to these success factors, it is important to identify the three key differentiators that give B2B marketing a distinctly different focus:

- **Weighting and prioritizing** – elements including personas, segments, demographics, etc.

- **Domain knowledge** – the expertise and overall sophistication of the prospect/customer

- **Level of the customer** – user, influencer, decision maker

Understanding these critical success factors and key differentiators will provide a mindset for the B2B marketing executive that will propel the organization toward SPPG.

Critical Success Factor #1: The Customer Controls Your B2B Brand and Position

While there is no universal agreement on the definition of brand, the core is simply how the market views your company—your reputation. It includes aspects such as what your firm is known for, where the market believes you have value or credibility, and your company's personality and culture.

Branding and positioning in B2B and B2C are a world apart. I'm a living case-in-point. I drink more Diet Coke than I do anything else. I have it stocked in my home fridge, in my work fridge, and I order it every day at lunch. The image of the Coke brand, for me as the customer, is defined entirely by the advertising, package design, and my experience with the taste. I have no personal relationship or connection with the organization itself, and yet I am entirely loyal to that brand. If the package is damaged I assume my local grocer dropped it while putting it out on the shelf. If it tastes bad when I order it at a restaurant, I blame the restaurant for not having the right mix of syrup and carbonated water. Coke has me pegged.

B2C companies invest millions to understand the various personas, segments, demographics, and geographical nuances to help them determine how to position and manage their brands to appeal to the faceless masses. In the retail category (e.g., Starbucks, Disney, Target), the brand is also impacted by elements such as the store (look, experience) and the people (knowledge, culture, and interactions).

In the B2B world, brand position is established with these same above-mentioned brand-building components. The major difference, however, is the *priority and weighting* these elements are assigned. The primary factor in determining this weighting is the impact a very few customers can have on the fate of the business. As you can see in the chart below, Williams Sonoma has the same amount of revenue as HCL; however, HCL has only 480 customers while Williams Sonoma has 33 million customers. Taking this a step farther, 75 percent of GE's sales come from only 80 customers, while the same percentage of sales at Williams Sonoma comes from 7 million customers. Getting this right—connecting with these few, key customers—can make the difference between branding Nirvana and losing your job.

Exhibit 1: B2C vs. B2B Customer Concentration (2010 sales and customer numbers)

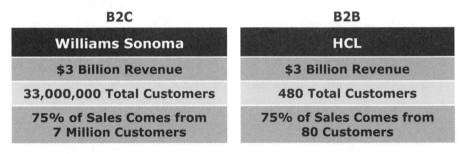

B2C	B2B
Williams Sonoma	**HCL**
$3 Billion Revenue	**$3 Billion Revenue**
33,000,000 Total Customers	**480 Total Customers**
75% of Sales Comes from 7 Million Customers	**75% of Sales Comes from 80 Customers**

In the B2B world, the people you are selling to are industry veterans who are usually subject matter experts. Simply put, they are living what you are selling. When HCL sells solutions to customers like Cisco, Merck, and Eli Lilly, the people who are evaluating and making the decisions are IT veterans in their respective industries for more than 20 years. When Harris Broadcast sells content distribution solutions to Dish Networks, Disney, McDonald's, and 7-Eleven, the people evaluating and making the decisions have more than 15 years in their respective industries. The expertise, level of complexity, layers of customer contacts, and overall sophistication of the prospect is exceptionally high.

In contrast, in a blind taste test in the B2C world, 90 percent of the population couldn't tell a $10 bottle of wine from a $100 bottle. Nor could they tell the difference between free tap water and a $5 Fiji bottled water. A sophisticated and highly emotional marketing and branding program can yield premium results when you're marketing something for which the buyer honestly can't differentiate the product.

In the B2B world, it's just the opposite. While customers may not know your specific offering, they usually know their industry better than those who supply it, and they know how to uniquely apply your product, solution, or service. They will scrutinize, compare, benchmark, test, and go to third parties and associations for references and validation.

Think about the ***domain knowledge*** level of the CIO who has worked in the financial services industry for 22 years. If you have IT solutions to serve this market, your company had better know his needs, priorities, environment, and requirements...and most of all, you better have peers (fellow CIOs) he can talk with about working with your firm. If you don't have this, a well-designed logo, powerful tagline, slick campaign, elaborate brochure, or Powepoint presentation will not overcome the lack of credibility to support a premium position. Too much is at risk in his world: security of bank assets, privacy issues, government compliance, the customer experience, and the CIO's reputation and career. In fact, CIOs consistently rate peer input as the number-one credible and trusted source, primarily due to their domain knowledge (source: 2011 survey by Geehan Group).

As a result, the most effective way to build or reposition a strong credible brand in B2B is through your current customers. It's how they describe their experience working with your company; it's what they say you successfully delivered (or where you fell short) that will ultimately determine your corporate brand position. And the higher level they are (user, influencer, decision maker), the more impact they have.

Tom Webster was the marketing leader at several firms prior to becoming CEO at Intesource. Webster concludes that in the B2B world, "The customers are your brand managers. They establish it and significantly impact it. And if you earn it, they can accelerate its evolution more effectively than anything else. Nothing boosts our position like a CFO (Intesource's key decision maker) sharing and endorsing the benefits of our solution or working with Intesource."

A little more than a decade ago, Indian service provider, HCL, broke into the U.S. market just like their Indian counterpart competitors—and all on the same "low cost" value proposition. Two things have changed since then. First, many of their U.S. competitors (IBM, HP/EDS, CA, Accenture, etc.) have set up significant operations in India (thus making their own cost structures more competitive). Second, HCL beefed up their capability to move up the value continuum by providing industry-leading offerings, shifting them from the Commodity Supplier positioning to that of a Reliable Supplier (a few years ago), to now being a Problem Solver. Here's their dilemma (brand gap): the companies who work with them are beginning to form their perception of HCL, but most prospective target companies are either unaware of HCL (little or no awareness of their added value) or have bundled them with the traditional Indian provider value proposition (as a low-cost provider).

Until perception catches up to reality, HCL will have discussions with customers and prospects anchored at (and, more importantly, margin expectations of) that of a Reliable Supplier vs. Problem Solver or Trusted Advisor—and it will have a financial impact on HCL's margins. This is where marketing and branding matters. HCL's global marketing leader Krishnan Chatterjee explained, "We have the proof points that can credibly support our position up the value continuum. My responsibility is to move the perception of the market to the reality of what we are capable of delivering to IT leaders around the globe." The scorecard will be the pipeline along with sales and margin growth vs. the competition.

The good news is it is easier to establish a brand if you have customers who can help effectively position the company by sharing their story and experience. Changing or transforming a brand is more difficult when you are trying to move up the value continuum.

For those who don't know HCL, a mix of marketing tactics is required to position the company in the desired higher position. The core marketing tactic must be customer-led references that definitively separate HCL from the traditional Indian "low cost" position and align them with the premium brands in their space. Secondly, there

Exhibit 2: The B2B Relationship Continuum—How Brand Perception Gaps Affect Margins

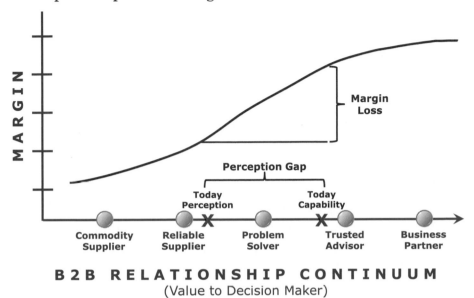

B2B RELATIONSHIP CONTINUUM
(Value to Decision Maker)

must be credible third parties (i.e., industry analysts like Forrester or Gartner) to validate the higher position. All this can then be supplemented by a messaging campaign that repeats and amplifies the position established by their most credible asset—their customers.

A logo, tagline, event sponsorship and/or sexy ad campaign will have little impact on success for B2B companies; and the higher you go up the value continuum, the more difficult success becomes exponentially, unless you have willing and enthusiastic decision makers to actively share their story on your behalf, and validation from respected third parties. This is where you'll have the most success branding or repositioning your company—it's also the fastest path.

Companies like Dell and Xerox established a strong brand position in the B2B space as reliable suppliers of IT hardware (PCs, laptops, and printers). The shift to become a credible brand as a higher-value supplier was so difficult they determined that buying brands with this higher-value continuum position made more financial sense (Dell with Perot Systems and Xerox with ACS).

Bottom line: In a B2B world, the few who control your fate in revenue and profitability—the decision makers within lead customers—also control the fate of your brand and gross margins. Actively engage these few parties; otherwise, branding and repositioning efforts will fail or, at best, take significantly longer. This is not the case with branding in the B2C world.

Critical Success Factor #2: Maximize Marketing's ROI

Part A: Move Up the Food Chain—The Decision Makers Control Your Fate

One of the fastest-growing large companies in the world is Palo Alto-based VMware. Their sales tripled from $600 million in 2006 to $2 billion in 2009, and they hit sales of $3 billion in 2010. This may be why they are Wall Street darlings. In addition to delivering high-growth, they are growing profitably and predictably relative to the competition.

What can B2B marketers learn from VMware's success? Most B2B companies spend marketing dollars targeting the wrong level of audience.

VMware's head of Global Strategic Partners, Scott Musson, believes starting at the top has been critical to their high growth/high margin success. He explained, "In our space, our competitors have been around for a long, long time (e.g., Microsoft). We don't have the luxury of branding ourselves to the entire planet. Nor do I believe it's even effective. We must maximize every marketing and sales dollar spent. And for VMware, as in other outperforming firms I've been a part of, the investment starts with the decision makers."

First and foremost, 75 percent of marketing budgets are targeted at the user/purchasing levels. Only 15 percent is spent at the influencer level, and sadly, only 10 percent is spent at the decision-maker level.

Let's examine this imbalance. Companies who have separated themselves from their benchmark competitors have a marketing budget spread that more closely resembles the following: 35 percent to the users/purchasing, 35 percent to influencers, and 30 percent to the decision makers. This shift is equivalent to approximately three times that of underperforming competitors. So clearly, rebalancing the marketing spend to target decision makers is important for success. B2B marketers who know and understand the breakdown of their spending can better allocate their budgets and make a huge difference in a short period of time.

Exhibit 3: Reallocation of Marketing and Sales Efforts and Resources

B2B Marketing Time/Money Allocation

	Typical	Optimal
Decision Maker Final authority/signature	10%	30%
Influencer Evaluation and due diligence of any potential purchase	15%	35%
User Those directly using the product or service	60%	30%
Purchasing Facilitate and govern buying protocols	15%	5%

Explanation: This represents marketing and sales budgets allocated to programs and initiatives that support the related buying segment or persona. This does not include time spent in Training and/or Customer Support.

How do you think the sales organization would feel about marketing if the number of qualified leads at the decision-maker level tripled? Penetrating the decision-maker level also shortens the sales cycle and more often shifts discussions from cost to value (yielding higher margins).

The objective of rebalancing is not to spend more. It's shifting the marketing budget to places where it will yield greater returns. That is why it is so important to analyze where your marketing budgets are going and spend strategically. Taking this view on branding and positioning provides insight to the CFO and offers a common reference point regarding the financial impact that the branding and positioning can have. When the number of customers that account for the majority of your revenue is small, it's important you weight your budgets accordingly.

Marketers who can justify the ROI on every dollar spent are the ones who become true partners within the organization and who catapult their credibility among the entire leadership team.

The quick litmus test is, "How effectively does marketing target and engage decision makers?" or "How do you personally connect with your top customer's decision makers?" An easy measure is to ask the sales team who they engage with at their top customers. If they don't engage the decision maker, the gun is smoking.

Part B: Make Your Current Customers Your Priority

Everyone gets excited when a major new customer is secured. There's a celebration, bells are ringing, and lots of recognition and rewards are doled out. It may even merit a personal call or note from the president.

Yet, how much celebration happens when a long-standing customer renews for the sixth straight year? Forget that they haven't bid out the work in three years (no competition = greater margin), and they are already in your system (low cost of support, faster payment = greater cash flow). What is marketing doing to celebrate and sustain these key wins?

It costs 3 to 5 times more to acquire a new account than it does to retain an existing customer. Getting your current customers buying more of your stuff means it's harder for them to leave you (increased switching cost), and current customers are much less likely to bid out your work (increasing profitability).

In 2009, the IT industry was hit hard by the economic downturn. HCL managed a 24 percent growth rate that year. Only one of their competitors grew during the same period (4 percent), and the rest of their competition were flat or fell below their previous year's sales. More than 70 percent of HCL's sales growth came from their current customers. Outperformers like HCL, Oracle, Wells Fargo and

Intesource invest more marketing dollars into existing account growth than new customer acquisition.

This is where marketing can help sales increase account penetration—aggressive marketing programs targeted at current customers. Too many companies miss this exceptional revenue opportunity. Think how many times your customers said, "I wish I'd known your company did that... I would have purchased from you." Marketing can change that.

By monitoring key metrics, you increase your chances for success:

- What are your retention rates?

- What is your percentage of penetration by offering? By account?

- What is the ROI of the offerings your customers are buying?

- What is the level of awareness of each of your offerings?

- What is the level of awareness with regard to company acquisitions and/or partnerships?

Once you have this key information, it's important that your area of the business focus on and evaluate the marketing spend to support maintaining your current customers. At the aforementioned companies, this is marketing's priority.

Exhibit 4: Maximizing the ROI on Marketing Budgets

Return on Marketing Spend

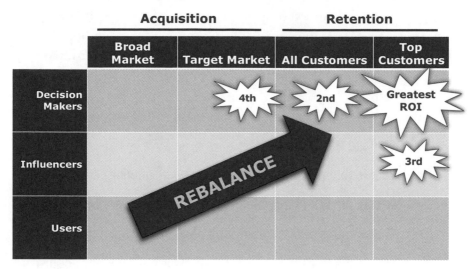

If you combine Parts A (*target the decision maker*) and B (*prioritize spend with current customers*), it quickly becomes apparent that your biggest opportunities lie within a few accounts, and a few specific people control your fate. This is true for companies like $3 billion HCL, where 75 percent of their revenue comes from just 70 customers or $20 billion GE Aviation, where 80 percent of their revenue comes from 50 customers, or a firm under $50 million like Intesource, where 80 percent of revenue comes from only 12 customers.

Start all your marketing plans here. This is where the greatest return on investment is made and where you will get support, and perhaps even more dollars, from the CFO.

Critical Success Factor #3: The Voice of the User ≠ the Voice of the Customer

Getting the right input from the market and acting on it will determine your mid- and long-term success. Marketing needs to immerse itself in this goal with absolute commitment.

Recently I met with the person who leads the "Voice of the Customer" (VOC) program for a $1.6 billion company in an industry in complete transformation. She proudly told me they had received more than 1,000 responses to their latest customer survey…and the numbers were great: more than 85 percent of the respondents were either satisfied or highly satisfied with the services offered. The problem here is that this firm only has a 68 percent retention rate. Most organizations try to predict retention rates based on customer satisfaction scores. The reality in B2B is *user satisfaction does not equal customer retention*. Here's why…

I asked her, "Of the more-than-1,000 respondents, how many decision makers completed and returned the survey?" Her response was, "Zero." Only three responses came from the influencer level. Virtually all the responses were from the user/purchasing level. Although these numbers are hard to believe, this is very common.

When we dug deeper, we learned that this company's margins, sales, and market share have been in decline for four straight years despite significant improvements in the User Satisfaction and NPS scores. While this balance may seem way out of line, the reality is that most executives don't fill out surveys and/or most companies don't have programs to get decision makers engaged in providing feedback.

Key question: Is your program a holistic "Voice of the Customer" or simply a "Voice of the User"?

I rarely see more than 20 percent weighting of decision makers and influencers combined in VOC programs. Due to this, many customer surveys and related programs are deceiving and misleading. Remember, most customers who leave a company, leave satisfied. (According to *Bloomberg Businessweek*, 60 percent of defecting customers describe themselves as "very satisfied" just before they leave—October, 2009.) The truth, unfortunately, is that user satisfaction does not equal customer retention.

Customer feedback must be separated by level to understand and align with the market needs to drive great retention, predictability, and insight.

A great example of how a company secures input from all levels within its customers' organizations is Oracle, and their multiple executive customer program initiatives led by SVP and Chief Customer Officer Jeb Dasteel. Oracle is committed to securing input and feedback from all levels.

Exhibit 5: Oracle consolidated and then tiered their feedback groups—standardizing the behaviors/input across each, and adopting a pyramid structure with each level.

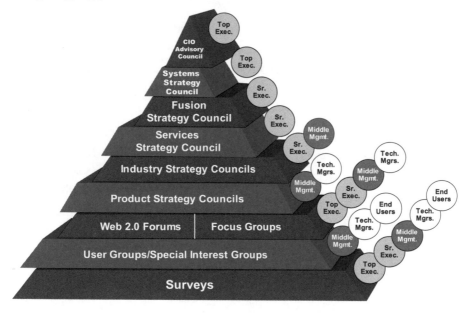

When Oracle has directly engaged with decision makers of a particular client, that client's retention rate was more than 20 percent greater than when Oracle did not have that level of relationship.

Oracle not only gauges the client's satisfaction, but also includes the client in key dialogues, ideation, and input opportunities. That gives decision makers a seat at the table to guide Oracle's direction. The partnership approach Oracle launched in 2004 has significantly separated it from its competitors.

Says Oracle's Dasteel, "While user relationships and their input are critical to our success, it is only one view. Without the engagement and insight of decision makers, we would be lacking whole categories of customer feedback and opportunities for collaboration."

User insight is valuable for product or service improvement, but it will not guide long-term success or predictability. Firms must engage at all levels but center on the decision maker to achieve sustainable, predictable, and profitable growth.

In the B2C arena, the user is usually the decision maker. I'm thirsty; I buy and drink a Coke. If I like the experience, I choose to buy another. Customer satisfaction is a very effective tool for repeat business in B2C. It's not that simple or straightforward in B2B, where there may be only hundreds of users, dozens of influencers, and perhaps a single decision maker—with whom most suppliers have little or no relationship.

Although it is comfortable to approach and engage users, they are just "table stakes." They cannot change the game. Most companies over-engineer their products to satisfy user requests but decision makers cannot justify the added investment. Therefore, the new products do not get purchased. By approaching the decision makers, marketers can determine exactly what will be purchased.

Bottom line: Be sure to start all VOC programs with the decision maker. That's where the war is won. Separate and analyze all VOC feedback by three levels: user, influencer and decision maker. This will give you a much more accurate view of where you stand with each important group.

Critical Success Factor #4: Applying the Right Program to Drive Leads and Sales

Marketers are open to new ideas and trying different approaches. This is a wonderful attribute. Every marketing leader must make sure these activities have defined objectives and measureable success criteria.

Remember when direct mail was the "shiny new toy?" About 20 years ago, a highly respected marketing executive sponsored a premium plan which had all the elements of an award-winning direct mail campaign. The program won several awards in marketing and industry circles. He was proud of the fact that it was an incredible success. Their original objective was to target their top 15 accounts and top 15 prospects in order to increase the number of "major accounts." Well, they went from 15 to 13 top accounts. In the end, the program lacked depth, substance, and relevance. But because of the awards and buzz, he went ahead and approved a similar campaign for the following year. When the CEO and sales leader found this out, the program was immediately halted. This person's credibility plummeted, and it took him years to earn it back.

Examples of pricey campaigns with no ROI can be found in many legacy programs: within a $1 billion company, 25 percent of its marketing budget was allocated to booths and sponsorships at more than 100 trade shows/conferences a year. The CEO recently asked for the ROI of these events. Not surprisingly, they were unable to associate a single deal with more than 80 of these events. They couldn't even name one specific deal that had resulted from the trade shows where they exhibited, although the objective of these events was to drive revenue and leads.

Naturally the CEO asked, "Why are we still going?" The answer: "Because we have always done them." The reality is the attendees of these trade shows are predominantly end-users. Rarely were influencers and/or decision makers part of these events. They now go only to the 10 conferences that include the influencers and decision makers—and they go with much more commitment, focus and investment. Quality in number of leads has been boosted significantly, along with much higher awareness among decision makers. There is now a strong ROI and a robust pipeline.

Today, there are so many shiny new toys—blogging, online communities, Twitter, webinars, mobile apps, etc. I'm a huge fan of these tools when applied appropriately. Before allocating the time and money, it is imperative to make sure you do the homework—determine whether this is where your influencers and decision makers are landing and participating. The next new thing can create a lot of excitement, but in the end, you are the one who needs to make sure the team is first and foremost delivering results (qualified leads, etc.).

We find legacy programs within many companies aren't delivering returns. These are highly redundant programs (surveys that ask the same questions from various parts of the organization, for example), or initiatives that are thrown together at the last minute (reactive). The result is usually a lot of activity, stress, errors, and very little impact on the original goal. The challenge for marketers is to truly take time to think about the few programs that will generate consistent results. (See Exhibit 6.)

Exhibit 6: Aligning Marketing Programs with Key Stages and Customer Levels

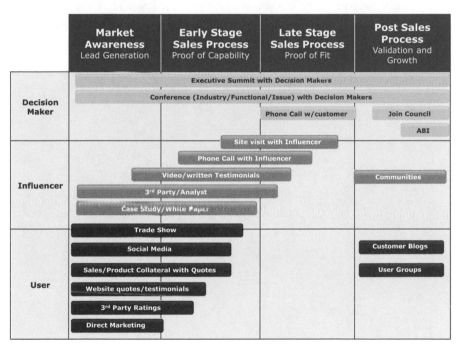

	Market Awareness Lead Generation	Early Stage Sales Process Proof of Capability	Late Stage Sales Process Proof of Fit	Post Sales Process Validation and Growth
Decision Maker	Executive Summit with Decision Makers			
	Conference (Industry/Functional/Issue) with Decision Makers			
			Phone Call w/customer	Join Council
				ABI
Influencer		Site visit with Influencer		
		Phone Call with Influencer		
		Video/written Testimonials		Communities
	3rd Party/Analyst			
	Case Study/White Paper			
User	Trade Show			
	Social Media			Customer Blogs
	Sales/Product Collateral with Quotes			User Groups
	Website quotes/testimonials			
	3rd Party Ratings			
	Direct Marketing			

Bottom line: Evaluate all your programs. There should be no sacred cows. You should include sales leaders to work through this process to get their support. Keep it as simple as possible. Plan the work and then work the plan.

Summary

By applying these concepts and truly following the tenets specific to B2B, you will catapult your credibility, impact, and longevity. Additionally, you will solidify leadership's understanding of the financial impact and value the marketing organization can bring to the B2B world.

International Study for Business Markets (ISBM) Executive Director Ralph Olivia summarizes it best saying, "Building brand awareness and credibility are 'Job One' for B2B marketing leaders." And having the tangible and financial proof that drives top and bottom lines results is a must.

On the softer side, following these principles will assist you in getting buy-in and team alignment, resulting in stronger cross-functional relationships. And again, these roads will ultimately lead to sustainable, predictable, profitable growth and earning marketing leaders a much deserved long-term "seat at the leadership team table."

B2B AND SOCIAL MEDIA

Social media is one of the latest and hottest tools for engaging customers, and B2B companies around the world are jumping on the bandwagon. A March 2011 survey by *B2B Magazine* found that 93 percent of B2B companies are using social media to some extent. But how effective is social media for engaging customers—and executive customers in particular—and can it deliver an ROI that justifies the investment in time and money?

When I sent the draft of this book out for my trusted peers to review, many people asked me a similar question, "What's the role of social media in the B2B world?" This is a new frontier and is changing very rapidly. My perspective on social media is cautious at this point, and I believe it will increase its impact faster than most realize. Beyond that, the only way to properly address this topic is to invite a recognized and respected social media guru to share his thoughts.

So I asked Paul Dunay, an award-winning B2B marketing expert, to answer this question and others I received. Paul is the chief marketing officer of Networked Insights, a leader in social media analytics, and author of four "Dummies" books on social media marketing: *Facebook Marketing for Dummies* (Wiley 2009), *Social Media and the Contact Center for Dummies* (Wiley Custom Publishing 2010), *Facebook Advertising for Dummies* (Wiley 2010), and *Facebook Marketing for Dummies 2nd edition* (Wiley 2011).

Paul, what is the state of social media today for B2B companies?

Paul Dunay: This is really the second or third year of social media becoming a mainstream phenomenon, with Facebook the movie, Mark Zuckerberg being named *Time*'s Man of the Year, and LinkedIn's highly successful IPO. So, that's why you see a lot of B2B companies experimenting with social media.

When you look at some of the stats, it is amazing how pervasive social media has become in the B2B marketing mix in such a short period of time. *B2B Magazine* found that 72 percent of B2B marketers are using LinkedIn, 71 percent are using Facebook, and 67 percent are using Twitter.

The next question is: What are they doing with all of this? What's the strategy behind that? I think the answer to that is "experimenting." We're still in a phase that I'd like to call "social science experiments." Social media may or may not tie to a business objective, and it may or may not show the results B2B companies are hoping for. It's a new form of media, and B2B marketers have to do some experimentation to find out whether and where it's going to fit in their particular organization.

What forms of social media are available to B2B companies?

Dunay: At its highest level, there are four choices. Think of them as quadrants.

One quadrant contains blogs and micro blogs, which are long and short forms of the same tool to publish information. Then you've got a quadrant with social networks and forums. To demystify social networks, it's helpful to think of them as simply better, newer versions of the online forums, such as The Well and UUNet that have been around for years. In the early forums, you asked a question and you got an answer. Now, social networks have been taken to a whole new level—you can share your friends, your likes and dislikes, etc. These are the traditional forums on steroids.

In a third quadrant, you have sharing technologies, things like Flicker, YouTube, UStream, SlideShare, and Scribd. These are services that allow you to share files, photos, PowerPoints, PDFs, and videos. I consider them enabling technologies for blogs, micro blogs, and social networks.

And in the last quadrant, you've got the more experiential stuff like Second Life—virtual worlds and multi-player games that are becoming very popular. I wouldn't put a lot of credence on those, especially in the B2B sense.

What's the typical mix in B2B companies?

Dunay: It depends on the company, but I think there are a few fundamentals. Micro blogging is becoming a fundamental. The blog is a fundamental. Taking part in some sort of social networking is critical. Then there are some enabling technologies. What are you sharing? Are you sharing videos? Then it's a service like YouTube. Are you sharing slides? Then maybe it's SlideShare.

The problem is that this mix of social media is assembled pretty quickly on the fly in a lot of companies. Many B2B firms are experiencing this rush of experimentation that feels like a morass.

How can companies avoid creating that morass?

Dunay: It's advisable to do a few things, do them really, really well, and not go too far beyond that. Try to keep your focus narrow and sharp.

When you think about participating in social media, it's good to think of it in two levels. In Level 1, you set up what I call an "embassy presence." You use this for typical broadcast communication, putting out press releases, white papers, etc. Level 2 is the higher level that depends on a target you want to engage that makes sense for your company. So, maybe it's talking to analysts, or maybe it's talking to the press, or maybe talking to unhappy customers and trying to make them happy again. There are multiple Level 2 strategies—which ones you adopt will determine how you want to engage your audience and which will work best for you.

Is it realistic for small and large B2B companies to use social media to engage and sell executive customers?

Dunay: Well, let's pull this question apart. Are B2B decision makers using social media? Unfortunately it's the same old answer: it depends. I can say for sure that the technology and telecom industries have the highest percentage of decision makers using social media. I wouldn't say CEOs, but certainly senior vice presidents and CIOs are taking part in social media in a very active way. But if you're a ball bearing manufacturer, are your customer decision makers using social media? Common sense suggests they probably are not. But somebody in the customer company's communications function or in their support function may be.

The second part of this question is about whether there are differences between small and large companies. I actually think you've got a lot of small B2B companies mixed in with the large companies. It's a little bit like what we saw in the Dot.com Era, when little start-ups like Amazon.com decided to try selling books online and ended up taking down established brick-and-mortar companies. You've got some very, very small businesses creating big reputations and getting big followings vis-à-vis social media, moving into the space before some of the very large companies.

I think this dynamic has been changing in the last year or so. You've got some large companies figuring it out. What's interesting is it's hard to tell the difference between small and large companies on social media. Small companies don't look so small in social media if they have a fairly large presence and a good following.

How do you get funding for social media initiatives in a B2B company?

Dunay: The politically correct answer is you put together a business case, run it up the flagpole, and get a bunch of people to salute. But the real way social media initiatives get funded is by experimenting with some disposable funds and seeing how it goes.

There are ways to experiment within a B2B organization where it isn't so hard to get funding. Maybe you grab a few dollars from a budget that's got some extra money or roll the cost into some other event. Social media initiatives are not that expensive. You can set up a Wordpress blog for free, share a photo on Flickr for free, and start a Facebook page for free.

You start with very low funding and get some experience before you go after the budget needed to launch social media in a "big bang" sort of way.

What about staffing for social media?

Dunay: Again, there's a politically correct answer and the short cut. You can try to get approval to hire dedicated employees and all that entails, or you can build a virtual staff.

When I first staffed for social media at BearingPoint and then Avaya, it was all virtual. Social media was the second or third job for everybody who worked with me. And that still works: recruit a team of people who are willing to participate on the side. At Avaya, I put together a virtual team of seven people from seven different disciplines, sales, communications, interactive, legal, alliances, etc. We all brought something a little different to the table, we all shared the responsibility, and we were able to make decisions and keep each other informed.

What's the best way to run the social media organization in a B2B company?

Dunay: I think there are two good structures for social media. One is a hub and spoke model with a clear leader, and the other is a network of individuals. The former, with one individual mainly responsible for social media, is much better. That way, when somebody says, "We need to do some social media for this new product," everybody knows where to turn as opposed to it being a "jump ball."

What are the best ROI opportunities using Social Media for B2B?

Dunay: Okay, 93 percent of B2B marketers are using social media, and of them, 68 percent don't know or can't measure their social media ROI. That's a shocking statistic, and I think it's because most B2B companies are too focused trying to find a way to come up with one ROI that encompasses all this media.

Everybody's got a different social media mix. So, how are you going to find a tool that's going to discern your mix and pull in all the data and all the stats across all the disparate media, and boom, calculate out an ROI at the push of a button? It's just not possible. We need to stop thinking about tools and start thinking about the right approaches. Look at companies that have done a great job with social media, like Dell with the very popular Dell Outlet Twitter feed. We should be thinking about how to use social media to sell excess phones or ball bearings or overstock or end-of-life materials and parts.

Another area where there's a good ROI is around communities. SAP has a very large social media community of about 1.2 million people from around 10,000 companies. They've got 100,000 members who are creating something like 3.5 million blog posts. Great ROI, too; SAP reports support calls going down and customer sales going up!

Another great approach is social customer support. This is something that I was working with Avaya on for two years, and I think there's a very, very strong ROI. When you have customers who are angry or upset with you, and they're taking it out on the social networks, you not only want to find them, but you want to surprise and delight them with great customer service to bring them back into the fold. The cost of acquiring a new customer in B2B is always quite high, so if you think about the cost of acquiring a new customer versus saving one that you've identified using social media, it doesn't take a rocket scientist to calculate the ROI.

Where is social media going in the B2B market in the next three years?

Dunay: It's hard to say where social media is going in B2B, but I can say where B2B is going to go in social media. I think over the next three years you're going to see continued experimentation. That means B2B executives are going to be in a constant state of catch-up for the next couple of years, especially if they haven't started yet. I don't say that to scare you, rather I say it to prompt experimentation to see if these new mediums will work for your company.

What should a B2B company do to get started in Social Media?

Dunay: The first place to get started is to create social media guidelines for your organization. If there is a corporate code of conduct that needs to be adapted for social media—great; if there is no code of conduct, create that first. Don't say bad things about your customers; don't mention big new client wins that might constitute a forward-looking statement about a public company. It's common sense, but for some reason with social media, common sense isn't always so common.

Then, try some social media tactics and see how they work with your company. Start a blog on your website. A blog is like a Swiss Army knife; you can connect the posts on the blog to the big social networking sites, such as Twitter, Facebook, and LinkedIn. A blog can serve as a content hub, and all social media depends on content. So I'd like to leave you by saying that you need a robust plan to generate the content needed to fill these media vessels. Social media feeds on content.

CASE STUDIES

HCL Improves Go-To-Market Strategy through Executive Customer Programs

*H*CL Technologies is a multi-billion-dollar global IT services firm that has grown by more than 20 percent annually during the past five years. The company has widely been considered a "transformational outsourcer" focused on delivering both innovation and value creation for customers. This concept stemmed from the company's ability to create and build an integrated portfolio of services offerings that includes software IT solutions, remote infrastructure management, engineering and R&D services, and business process outsourcing (BPO) services.

How HCL maintains the position of "transformational outsourcer" is not as widely known. In 2007, revenues for the company were $1.4 billion and it was considered one of the fastest growing firms in the world. For HCL to continue this aggressive growth, the company would have to identify—and aggressively pursue—new opportunities with existing customers, as well as with new prospects in both established and emerging markets.

The leadership team knew it had to identify ways to solidify company growth moving forward. The team was unsure how to project what their customers' needs, wants, and expectations would be several years in advance.

The HCL leadership team determined in order for its IT solutions to be truly "transformational" they must add significant customer value. They also determined that "high touch" executive customer programs were the best way to gain a deep understanding of customers' business drivers and the major issues affecting the industries in which they operate. The leadership team decided to create a forum to receive regular feedback and insights from customers to further strengthen and better align HCL's solutions with the market.

The Customer Advisory Council

HCL's Customer Advisory Council (CAC) was formed in 2008 and initially consisted of 80 Fortune 500 C-level customer executives and thought leaders who met regularly to exchange ideas, experiences, and best practices. The CAC members often provided HCL's leadership team with significant insight on new and interesting industry trends, as well as helpful guidance around fluctuating business priorities.

Three years later, HCL's CAC programs have proven to be very successful from a number of perspectives and this initiative has expanded to include four separate but highly complementary programs. In North America, one program consists of customer CIOs who advise HCL on management processes, and another program with CTOs that focuses on research and development initiatives. HCL also has two other CAC groups in Europe and Asia-Pacific.

In 2010 HCL continued to demonstrate rapid growth with recorded revenues of $3.3 billion, a success it believes is directly attributable to the CAC programs launched in 2008.

The Case for CAC

The role of HCL's CAC has significantly impacted the company's strategic business plan and serves as a platform to:

1. Improve strategic relationships with key decision makers in HCL's top 80 accounts

2. Enhance the company's ability to sustain, cross-sell, and grow large strategic accounts

3. Validate that HCL is launching the right products and services at the right times

4. Create a reference management system populated with key C-level customers

5. Elevate HCL's positioning in customers' minds to that of a truly valued business partner, not merely a vendor

1. Understanding Customer Needs

HCL's CAC program provides early warnings of shifts in customer needs and emerging technologies. It also helps the company better understand how to approach and serve customers across industries and markets. Additionally, it is a platform to connect prospective customers with existing customers, and allows for candid discussions about HCL's services and capabilities as well as its successes and (sometimes) failures (or mistakes).

By establishing a formal council, HCL has been able to determine the optimal timing and business practices around launching new services and strategic initiatives. It also helps HCL validate new service platforms, evaluate new and emerging markets HCL is looking to pursue, and properly allocate resources to client accounts based on the clients' own views and feedback. Having tremendous involvement from CAC members in shaping new services has also helped with cultivating them as early adopters of the services, generating some additional revenue, and stimulating confidence and acceptance in the market.

2. Innovation

HCL's CAC brings together executive customers biannually with a combined 300 years' experience across global IT services industries. After five successful meetings, the council suggested HCL begin a technology council for the CTOs and engineering and R&D heads within their organizations. In 2010, a parallel council was initiated and to date there have already been two tech council meetings completed. The technology council provided invaluable feedback on the company's product portfolio management and its long-term product strategy. Advisory council members drive the agenda and propose hot topics within the technology and engineering sector that are most relevant to their individual organizations.

For the first time, these programs encouraged HCL's customers to begin suggesting ways in which the company can transition from being a reliable supplier to a strategic problem solver. For example, council members asked the company to build stronger middle management teams to collaborate with them as they seek to solve their problems.

Value Continuum

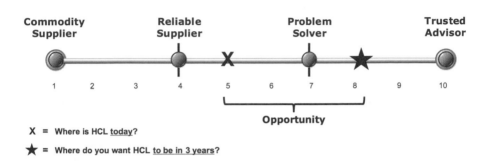

X = Where is HCL today?

★ = Where do you want HCL to be in 3 years?

Further, executive customers provided input on the future investment and strategic goals of the company in working sessions held during CAC meetings that asked them what they would do "If you were the CEO of HCL."

The result: more Fortune 500 companies are partnering with HCL for mission-critical projects, including recent business wins of Eli Lilly, Xerox, and Merck.

3. Execution

While the CAC program today is very comprehensive, HCL was initially tasked with determining how it would pique the interest of their executive customers to participate. The leadership team had to identify ways to assure prospective members it would not be self-promoting.

To overcome that hurdle, Shami Khorana, President of HCL America, serves as the executive sponsor of the council. He spends two full days in all advisory council meetings and oversees all communications with council members. In addition, current advisory council members call prospective members to answer any questions they might have and explain the strategic nature of the council.

The second challenge was an internal one. Being such a large organization, HCL is highly decentralized, and demonstrating the tangible benefits of council involvement to various HCL stakeholders was not easy.

4. Leveraging the CAC Relationships

HCL's flagship event, the Global Customer Meet (GCM), is held every 18 months and brings together not only HCL customers but also global business executives and prospective customers to spur new thinking on the most important IT, business, and social issues.

GCMs have featured such celebrated speakers as President Bill Clinton, Gary Hamel, Malcolm Gladwell, top-tier CEOs, and, of course, many CAC members who share their stories and experiences with other IT leaders. As one CAC member who presented shared, "When a company like HCL can get so many C-level executives up in front of hundreds of their peers, it's very powerful." There is no doubt HCL has earned the trust and respect of the CAC members who so enthusiastically opt-in to help make the company a success.

In terms of business, the event accelerates cross-sell and up-sell opportunities both with and for HCL's customers. It also drives awareness of HCL's continuous expansion of core capabilities like cloud computing, virtualization, mobility, and other industry-specific offerings. It is a tremendous "assist" in moving the market perception (brand) of HCL from reliable supplier to strategic problem solver, which differentiates it from other Indian IT services firms.

5. Tangible Results

While there is no way to fully quantify the successful results HCL has experienced in large part due to the CAC programs, there are a few data points that can help tell part of the story. To date, some of the business results of HCL's CACs include:

- Retention of all advisory council customers since its inception in 2008.

- A 200 percent increase in the number of HCL accounts willing to provide references.

- From 2007 to 2008, the satisfaction of CAC customers increased at twice the rate of other customers, from 68 percent to 88 percent.

- 30 percent of CAC members have agreed to support HCL in its thought leadership initiatives.

- CAC customer revenues have grown an average of 58 percent vs. 33 percent overall from 2008. Over a three-year period, the advisory council also supported 300 percent growth in the number of $10 million accounts, 200 percent growth in $20 million accounts, and 230 percent growth in $50 million accounts.

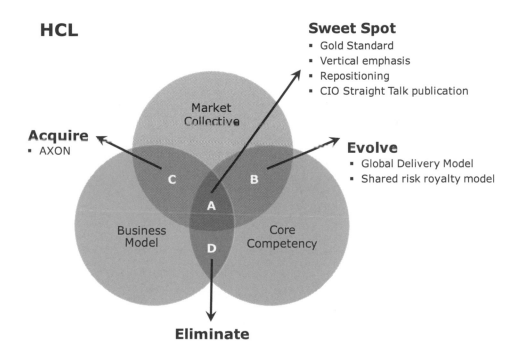

Other areas the CAC has assisted HCL ideation, direction, and planning are illustrated in the Venn diagram below:

Perhaps the best quantifying data to relay the success of the CAC program is HCL's 2010 revenues of $3.3 billion, representing an increase of more than $2 billion (the CAC programs and its members played a major role in this success). These numbers speak for themselves and truly illustrate the benefits of creating a non-threatening and noncommercial forum for executive customers to express their views freely and help strengthen customer relationships.

Overall, the CAC has enabled HCL to increase its revenues, deepen relationships, and raise customer satisfaction levels. It has also created a pool of references for large deals and enhanced the retention rates of strategic accounts currently leveraged at HCL's Global Customer Meet, as well as other private and public events.

These milestones, while impressive, are only the continuation of HCL's journey. HCL recently announced its goal of reaching $6 billion in revenue by 2014 and it knows the success of programs like the CAC will be critical toward helping it reach this goal.

Khorana shares his keys to a successful council:

1. *Management commitment*—both time and support.

2. *No selling*—it is not about self-promoting or closing deals.

3. *Collaborative agenda*—member-driven and interactive.

4. *The right customers*—not just big, but committed customers.

ORACLE®

ORACLE'S CUSTOMER PROGRAM ARCHITECTURE DRIVES ALIGNMENT— AND RESULTS

"It is through continuous customer interaction that we're able to relentlessly refine and retune our own best practices to meet evolving customer needs."

—Jeff Henley, Chairman of the Board, Oracle

The emergence of the Internet in the mid-90s presented a serious challenge for software companies. Early entry in the new market meant undertaking radical business-model transformation long before the market had been tested or matured. And, for those who made the gamble, what recourse would they have if the market failed to develop?

One of the companies that went all in, and stayed all in, was Oracle Corporation. In 1997 Oracle co-founder and CEO Larry Ellison placed a big bet on the future of the Internet by directing his company to write software for the new Internet environment and to make application software its core business. Convinced of his vision for Oracle's dominance in the Internet-application software industry, Ellison raised the stakes when he acquired PeopleSoft for $10.3 billion in 2005.

Today, Oracle is the world's leading supplier of information-management software and complete systems.

Turning Point

"The defining moment for us was the PeopleSoft acquisition," recalls Jeb Dasteel, Oracle's SVP and chief customer officer (CCO). "It was a very contentious process by definition. We had a lot of PeopleSoft customers that were extremely upset."

However, the issue wasn't product based. It was customers' perception that Oracle wasn't customer focused.

Prior to the acquisitions, Oracle was viewed as a sales- and engineering-driven organization. "And in many ways, behaviorally, quite the opposite of PeopleSoft, which was perceived as very warm and fuzzy—very customer focused," says Dasteel.

Oracle executives knew they had to undertake a significant customer-retention effort throughout the organization to convince PeopleSoft's customers to remain loyal. And they knew that effort had to be more about deeds than words. So they did two very important things: first they decided to retain the PeopleSoft brand and revive the J.D. Edwards brand (which had been retired when J.D. Edwards merged PeopleSoft in 2003); and second, they created an integrated set of programs focused entirely on customer retention and the customer's success.

Oracle Customer Acquisition and Engagement Timeline

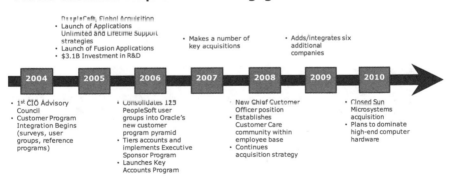

$$\left[\begin{array}{c}\textbf{\textit{"A key success factor of the PeopleSoft}}\\\textbf{\textit{acquisition hinged on how effectively we proved}}\\\textbf{\textit{our commitment to these new customers."}}\end{array}\right]$$

—Jeb Dasteel

Building the Customer Roadmap

The PeopleSoft acquisition was the stimulus for change, but the vision came from Charles Phillips, then Oracle's co-president (retired 2010). Phillips recognized the urgent need to transform the organization's relationships with its customer base.

In preparation for the acquisition, Phillips tapped Dasteel to launch an integrated set of end-user, influencer, and decision-maker level customer programs. "While user relationships and their input are critical to our success, it is only one level," says Dasteel. "Charles had maintained a very clear vision of how important relationships are at every level of the decision chain." Without the perspective and insight of decision makers, we would be lacking "whole categories of customer input today." As part of the larger customer-care strategy, Oracle launched a CIO Advisory Council in October 2004. The idea was Phillips' and was based on the tight relationships he had formed with CIOs in his former role as a technology industry analyst.

Dasteel translated Phillips' vision into a customer care strategy focused on retaining PeopleSoft customers. This approach, also referred to as "the customer lifecycle," has evolved since its inception in 2004.

At the time, listening and engaging customers at high levels wasn't an Oracle strength. On a scale of 1 to 10 Dasteel says they were probably a 2. As a result, the inaugural CIO Advisory Council was "*painful!*"

"I remember scratching my head and thinking 'I'm not sure if I'm going to get another customer to come back,'" admits Dasteel. "We were good at pitching, but not very good at listening. It was a rough meeting, but fortunately that listening aspect of our relationship with customers has really exploded over the years." Happily, it turned out that customers were delighted just to have been invited to an attempt at a more strategic dialogue with them.

Oracle found that executive-level advisory councils were very different from the advisory councils they had been operating at the product level for many years. A product engineer could talk to you until they were blue about features and functionality, but Oracle had never consistently elevated the discussions to business-level dialogues. So this was a first.

Despite that painful first meeting, Oracle pressed on. The company deliberately focused on building CIO relationships and its executives improved their dialogue skills. Oracle also formalized a structure for customer feedback that allowed it to not only consolidate the 125 feedback groups it had acquired with PeopleSoft, but to add feedback groups at different levels across the organization. While it is a complex structure, it works for Oracle due to the high level of senior executive commitment and the company's programmatic approach.

Customer Feedback / Different Channels & Audiences:

Oracle consolidated and then tiered its feedback groups—standardizing the behaviors across each of them and adopting a pyramid structure with each level focused on a different time horizon.

Demonstrating the importance Oracle places on thoughtful customer interaction at all levels, Jeff Henley, chairman of the board, says, "Customer care and customer feedback intersect with customer strategy through constant dialogue. It is through continuous customer interaction that we're able to relentlessly refine and retune our own best practices to meet evolving customer needs."

Continuing the Journey: Engaging Directly with Key Customers

The PeopleSoft deal closed in January 2005 and Oracle timed the launch of its Applications Unlimited and Lifetime Support strategies, as well as Oracle's Fusion Applications, to coincide with the closing. In doing so, the company made the statement that they were going to maintain and build upon the products they had acquired, as well as create an innovative, forward-looking suite of new applications under their new brands.

The message to customers was backed by new product launches and a $3.1 billion investment in research and development. But it was complicated by a sales model that often required a dozen technical sales reps within an account—a significant increase from the four to six reps just a few years earlier.

Oracle addressed this challenge by implementing a formal opportunity management and account management program that allowed for selling in a more strategic way. The company also tiered its 340,000 accounts—labeling the top 196 as "key accounts." Each key account was assigned a key account director, who is responsible for day-to-day activity, and an executive sponsor, who owns the customer relationship at a senior executive level.

The executive sponsor is a one-on-one tool in Oracle's customer-engagement suite. The role exists solely to build relationships at the highest level and completely outside of any particular transaction.

> *"If you look today at who are our very best, our most loyal customers, and best references, it tends to be those who are most engaged. And the way they get actively engaged is through the structured customer programs we've built. Chief among those is advisory boards."*
>
> —Jeb Dasteel

"The reason this customer interaction is so effective on both the executive side as well as the traditional service channels is because Oracle executives and employees aren't just worried about problems that come up," says Oracle's Keith Block, executive vice president for North American sales and consulting. "They are looking to help customers with future growth as well. And if that includes looking out at the world and connecting Oracle customers with outside partners, that's what happens."

The account team and executive sponsor help customers to get the most out of their relationship with Oracle, " Don Imholz, vice president of information technology for Boeing Integrated Defense Systems, explained in Oracle's *Profit* magazine. "It's a mix of Boeing executives visiting Oracle and receiving briefings from the sales team, making sure that the agenda fits the needs of both parties, and Oracle executives coming here to get more immersed in the business and understand our needs."

At Oracle, every senior executive is involved with customers as an executive sponsor because, as Dasteel's measurement process reveals, "The best, most influential reference customers we have in the world are the ones with whom we have personal relationships."

Acting on Customer Input

"Partnership on paper means nothing. You really have to commit and engage, and both sides have to be able to expect that," says Block. This level of commitment is demonstrated at every level of the organization. In fact, Larry Ellison recently attended a recent council meeting, along with four members of the company's board.

Underscoring the importance of the customer programs is their overarching role in aligning the leadership team and Oracle's direction. "They are at the foundation of our success in so many areas: strategy, development of products and services, acquisitions, revenue growth, customer retention rates, and account penetration," says Dasteel.

Thomas Kurian, Oracle's executive vice president of development, adds: "Aligning our product strategy and direction around customer business objectives is core. We have built the breadth of product functionality so that customers can benefit from our innovation through enhanced business results. Customers are at the heart of our vision to deliver comprehensive product sets that meet business needs, minimize risk, and add business value."

One example of this is Oracle Insight, a service delivered by Oracle's Industries business unit. Oracle Insight was created in response to customer requests for help identifying opportunities for business value, to take advantage of the best practices exhibited by other customers, and to benchmark their performance against like organizations. Another example is Oracle's client-advisor program. This program, which was instituted at the direct request of Oracle's CIO advisory council, provides customers with an enterprise architect.

In addition to providing input to the product roadmap, Oracle's advisory councils validate the company's acquisition strategy. This is best illustrated by the build out of products and services aimed at key markets, including health sciences, retail, communications, utilities, public sector, and financial services. "We provide very complete systems for very specific industry needs because of the customer feedback we receive," comments Dasteel.

Creating Sustainable Results through a Culture of Competition and Governance

Unlike some companies that have vowed to become customer-centric, Oracle did not change its culture. Instead, it exploited its existing culture.

"People at Oracle are very competitive," states Dasteel. "If you can weave customer centricity into that competitive nature, you get a winning strategy. Imagine presenting various forms of customer satisfaction data across difference business units and encouraging teams to compete with one another on a customer success and loyalty basis."

How has that worked? "Amazingly," declares Dasteel, "especially if people can see the straight line from being customer-centric to increased revenue and increased profitability. If you can take someone down that path and get them to see that readily—then you're golden."

The way Oracle takes employees down this path is to integrate a customer-focused perspective into all they do. Structurally, Oracle created the position of chief customer officer (CCO), which Dasteel currently holds. "Our chief customer officer has become a key part of the Oracle transformation. The pay-off has been tremendous..." shared Charles Phillips.

Oracle Customers Engaged in Customer Programs vs. Those Not Engaged	
Overall Satisfaction Rating	24% Greater When Engaged in a Customer Program
Willing to Recommend	19% Greater When Engaged in a Customer Program
Continue Purchasing	25% Greater When Engaged in a Customer Program

Data supports Oracle's focus on relationships. A review of their top 400 accounts shows significant differences between customers involved in relationship programs and those who are not.

Oracle also created a network of employees in various functions, including sales, engineering, training, service and support, legal, and finance, which are charged with customer care. Dasteel describes this group as a community responsible for standardizing the behaviors, expectations, and roles and responsibilities associated with customer care.

Driving Oracle's Strategy, Direction, and Decision Making

Most importantly, however, is that customer data is shared widely throughout Oracle and used to make more informed and strategically aligned decisions. The impact of hearing directly from customers, and not from another employee who heard it from the customer, is crucial. "It gives us confidence in our convictions," says Dasteel.

Advisory councils not only allow Oracle's leaders and employees to hear straight from their customers, but to communicate directly with them as well—a critical task for a company whose culture is rooted in transparency and fast decision making. "Even if we don't have all the facts, we create clarity for the customer, for the investor, for the acquired company employees, for Oracle employees, and for third party observers," Dasteel says.

The Payoff

"Two." That's the rating on a scale of 1 to 10 that Dasteel gave Oracle five years ago with respect to listening to the customer. "Today," he says, "We're a solid 8 or 9."

As a result of listening, and an overarching architecture for customer focus, Oracle is seeing huge payoffs. Oracle's best customers are not only more committed, they play an integral role in Oracle's sales process as loyal advocates.

"It's magic," says Dasteel of the reference program which includes some of its largest customers. "If you look today at who are our very best, our most loyal customers, and best references, it tends to be those who are most engaged. And the way they get actively engaged is through the structured customer programs we've built," says Dasteel.

Chief among those programs is the CIO advisory council and related customer councils. Dasteel admits he could have created a reference program without the advisory councils and other programs, but that it would have been very difficult.

Through a systematic, long-term investment, Oracle has earned an incredible level of customer collaboration and trust. They create relationships that have nothing to do with a particular transaction. Dasteel shares, "It's to the point that those customers may not be completely thrilled with every single aspect of the product they recently implemented, but they are still willing to be strong references for us because of the relationship we've built. They are willing to put their reputation on the line endorsing us…and we take that trust very seriously." Data supports Oracle's focus on relationships. Of Oracle's top 400 accounts, 77 percent are involved in one or more customer programs. The revenue in those accounts is 13 percent higher than in non-participating accounts, and customer satisfaction is 24 percent higher.

In the end, however, results need to be reflected in shareholder value. When compared to other software firms since the customer transformation began, Oracle has clearly delivered—outperforming the Dow Jones, software industry as a whole, and their biggest competitors including Microsoft and SAP. Oracle total shareholder return from Jan 2005 to July 2011 was 139 percent, vs SAP at 48 percent and Microsoft at 1 percent (sources: Bernstein, Factset, Capital IQ, Yahoo Finance).

The Journey Continues

Where does Oracle go from here? They continue to listen and engage their customers.

Oracle is now in the process of launching a CFO advisory council that has two objectives. One is to get the CFO perspective on specific product categories such as business intelligence, governance, and risk and performance management. The second is to build relationships with CFOs who may be strong influencers within their organization.

Oracle's future will clearly be shaped by its customers as it continues to systematically combine all of its feedback into a single voice of the customer for alignment and decision making.

It is this voice that Dasteel says is critical to their customer engagement programs' success. "If I had to do it all over again I'd start by building the best possible system for collecting and reporting customer feedback. That builds credibility, one real 'voice of the customer' around which all other customer programs can be built."

Customer Discoveries by Jeb Dasteel

1. If we had never launched our full suite of customer programs, relying entirely on user-group input instead, we would be lacking whole categories of customer feedback.

2. If we bring customers to an advisory board setting and have a dialogue outside any transaction, it creates a relationship that trumps anything else happening in the account.

3. If Oracle had spent the last six years just focused on a reference program, we wouldn't have gotten very far. What has made the customer relationships work for us, in terms of loyalty and selling to other customers via references, is that we have very deliberately created a lifecycle that connects these customer programs with reference opportunities. A byproduct of Oracle's customer programs is that participating accounts are more satisfied, more loyal, and more referenceable.

Jeb Dasteel is SVP, chief customer officer at Oracle. Since 2004 Mr. Dasteel has run Oracle's Global Customer Programs. In 2008 he was appointed Oracle's first chief customer officer (CCO); in 2009 he was named Chief Customer Officer of the Year.

"THE **EAB** SHIFTED OUR MINDSET AND
HELPED US MOVE FROM A HARDWARE/
SOFTWARE BUSINESS
TO A MEDIA BUSINESS."

–Harris Morris, President, Harris Broadcast

*"The goal of the customer engagement program is
to enable BCD to transform the business—where we
innovate, how we position ourselves, and how we sell—
by aligning ourselves to what our most
influential customers want."*

—Harris Morris, President, Harris Broadcast

Turn on a television or a radio anywhere in the world. Chances are that the signal you receive is being broadcast with equipment from Harris Corporation's Broadcast Communications Division (BCD).

Harris became the leader in the broadcasting industry in 1957 when it acquired Gates Radio, which had introduced its first transmitter to what was then a fledgling radio industry in 1936. Major local radio stations such as WLW in Cincinnati, WJR in Detroit, and WOR in New York needed powerful systems to distribute Amo 'n' Andy and Groucho Marx on the airwaves. Harris delivered and sold to them all. Later, with the boom of the television market in the 50s and 60s, Harris leveraged relationships with radio broadcasters and began marketing its first line of VHF and UHF transmitters for television. The wave of growth continued, worldwide.

Throughout the '80s and '90s, the broadcast market continued to evolve on two fronts. The broadcast-transmission business moved from traditional analog transmission to digital transmission—first in the U.S. and then globally. Second, the broadcaster's world become more complex as broadcasters, now able to work on a digital platform, were challenged by their corporations to deliver newer, faster, and more dynamic content to a widening distribution network—and simultaneously drive diversifying ad sales.

To keep pace with market changes and faster development cycles, Harris BCD went on a buying spree. Between 1997 and 2007, 11 companies across the globe were acquired for almost USD $1 billion. The endgame? Position Harris as the leader in providing end-to-end products that support the content-delivery chain from production through distribution and transmission.

All seemed on track as the portfolio of solutions grew in sync with the overall market as customers worldwide moved to digital platforms. And yet, trouble was brewing. Like watching the waters slowly move up along a flood-swollen riverbank, Harris could see the implications to its business: customers' priorities were changing coupled with an increase in the presence of IT firms within the installed base.

Harris for its part had become a deeply siloed organization as a result of its acquisitions, each of which brought its own expertise, culture, and outlook on life. The engineers, developers, marketers, and sales reps from each group focused on the product they knew best. Few had a clear understanding of the value of the entire product portfolio, how to integrate solutions, and, most importantly, how to leverage relationships with customers to develop, market, and sell the entire portfolio.

In 2008 the division realized it needed to clearly understand top customers' directions and needed to validate solutions Harris was considering and developing. They also knew they needed to advance the business acumen and executive presence of the account teams.

Evolution of Television Technology

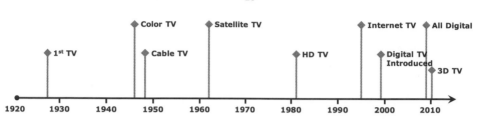

Source: Geehan Group research.

Harris Morris shares, "The speed of our industry was changing so rapidly that we needed to overhaul our planning process to match the velocity of our market to make sure we not only kept up but excelled in meeting our customers' needs and maintained our competing capability."

Beginning the Journey

The Harris sales organization engaged regularly with customers at the operational and user levels. The product teams had full lists of features and functions to add to the siloed product portfolio. What the leadership team realized was missing was tying the products and services together and delivering the value proposition at an executive level to the market. The leadership team needed to figure out the best approach to engage executive-level customers and begin the transformation of Harris.

Several paths to achieve executive-level engagement were considered, including a large-scale event, a series of road shows, and targeting Harris' major accounts. They were concerned, however, that this approach would lead to an audience at the operational level—the level that the sales organization engaged as part of the normal course of business—rather than the executive decision-making level.

After studying the needs of the company, they identified the path for success...

With this perspective in mind, Harris set out to form an Executive Advisory Board (EAB) coupled with an Executive Sponsored **Account Based Innovation** program (ABI). The EAB was designed as a forum

Executive Advisory Board Objectives		
Customer Engagement	**Strategy and Trends**	**Offerings**
• Identify, **build, and foster relationships** with market-leading organizations. • Understand processes, practices, and methods to **accelerate sales** in target accounts.	• **Identify emerging trends** and determine the timing, impact, potential business models, and operational changes necessary to succeed. • Understand where and **how to allocate resources** for success in the market.	• Understand the Harris **value proposition** to achieve greater penetration of end-to-end solutions. • **Identify future portfolio improvements** and innovations. • **Understand solution adoption** timing and impact.

for customer executives to connect with the BCD executive team and to provide market-based insights and clarity toward the development of company strategies, products, services, and resource priorities. The ABI program was established to extend the relationships developed in the advisory board to individual accounts, whereby a BCD executive works one-on-one with the customer executive to establish team-to-team relationships to drive account insight, solutions, and sales.

The Executive Advisory Board

When it came to recruiting the inaugural members of the EAB, two seasoned sales executives that held the strongest relationships with the major media accounts were brought in. Through the efforts of a very professional recruiting process involving key BCD executives, the team was successful in recruiting 13 executives from their top customers. No small feat given the fact that these were executives from marquee companies like CBS, Fox, Warner Bros., Comcast, Discovery, and Turner. An inaugural EAB meeting was hosted in July 2008.

From the start, the program has been a success. The inaugural meeting was held at a carefully selected venue—one that provided an intimate setting, comfortable and serene surroundings, and accommodating business meeting environment spanning two days. Spouses of the customer executives were invited and hosted separately. The business discussions were focused on industry challenges, trends, and the implications for transformation to digital platforms.

Harris continues to engage the group collectively every six to nine months. Meetings continue to be held in off-site locations to allow both the Harris BCD team and the EAB members to think outside their day-to-day operations. Board members have come to appreciate the broad spectrum of representation on the board and benefits of learning from their peers. They appreciate the candor of the Harris team and identify the interaction between members and Harris' openness and willingness to listen.

Harris BCD has summed up the value and benefits of the program into three categories: strategic transformation, product decisions, and customer relationships.

Strategic Transformation

An early insight gained by Harris was that customers think about their business differently than how Harris is organized. Customers organize and deliver around workflows and process flows, and they needed Harris to think and act around file- (content) based workflows.

This insight was profound.

> *"The real benefit, if you do it right, is that you get to know your customers better than your competitors do. You get early insights, you hear about their strategies. And you turn this insight into action.*

—Brad Turner, Vice President, Strategy and Marketing

It became clear to Harris Morris and the team that the company must organize around the demands of the market and deliver solutions that add value across business processes. This insight first led to the creation of the Harris CTO council—an internal group of technology leaders tasked to look across the organization and determine where workflows and interoperability between products needed to be improved to meet market demands. This council became the cornerstone for BCD to take market-based requirements and technology trends in to the organization for cross-functional implementation.

The EAB's insight later led to the organizational changes to create the "WIN" business unit. The WIN unit is comprised of the workflow, infrastructure, and networking products and services, and aligns with the market demands.

> *"The EAB augmented our recognition that a customer focus across the enterprise was needed. They recognize that we provide more than hardware/software solutions. We are a media business helping customers facilitate returns on content. That's the epiphany of an enterprise-wide solution."*
>
> —Harris Morris, President

Market Insight ——> Strategic Planning

Another key observation gained by the BCD team was that the collective input from this group provides invaluable insights to BCD's strategy. But, timing for the input was often out of synch with the company operating plans. Once the fiscal year begins, changing course is like

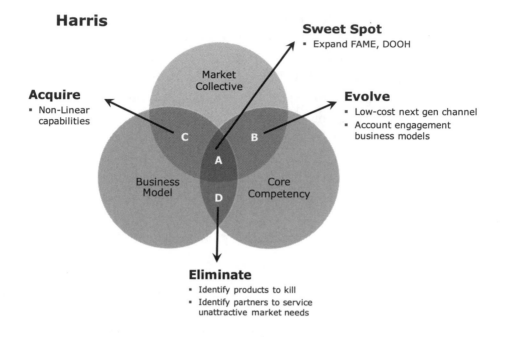

changing tires on a moving car—it's really hard to make a course correction happen. Brad Turner, vice president, marketing and strategy, was brought in by Harris Morris to organize the company's business strategy process and approach, and he quickly realized that it's imperative to align the EAB with the strategic planning process. With that, a new timing and sequence has been formed so the beginning and end of the strategic planning cycles are aligned with the key engagement touch points with the EAB members.

> ## "Sequencing and aligning the EAB calendar with our corporate planning cycle allows us to achieve market alignment."

—Brad Turner, Vice President, Strategy and Marketing

Product Decisions

Prior to the EAB, development of new products was primarily driven by new technology requirements. Product teams would work toward feature and functional requirements from personal insight or one-off customer visits. Aligning with customers through the EAB has elevated the product level discussions to those that are more strategic and ultimately more valuable to customers and Harris. EAB members provide insights to cross-functional workflows, interoperability, product retirement, and new industry standards that impact the success and future of the Harris product portfolio.

> *"The reality is that the EAB is a powerful way to empower managers with the confidence and belief in what they are doing to make changes that will get the job done. It helps us focus on what's working and gives us the confidence to kill what's not."*

–Harris Morris, President

In terms of innovation, the EAB works with Harris at multiple levels, and has resulted in substantial process improvements in the product-development lifecycle. The members of the EAB set the strategic priorities that are emerging in the market. As the definition and market sizing exercises unfold, these EAB members align individual subject-matter experts throughout their organizations to provide clearer and more finite definition of the product requirements. A great example is how the EAB members identify three distinct areas of need: content, channels, and advertising business models. Harris took these three areas and created "working groups" to vet out solutions.

Members stepped forward and provided subject-matter experts from their respective firms to work with Harris, and these teams identified a total of 13 separate innovations. These 13 innovations were brought back to the EAB for prioritization based on high-level scoping and business value. It was quickly determined that more than half of the solutions should *not* be developed, and three solutions rose to the top as high priorities.

> **"We've made mistakes when we thought we were smarter than the customer... making future decisions on their behalf, trying to solve problems they don't have, and fixing things they don't need us to fix. Fortunately, these customers are pretty direct. They know what works and we've stopped trying to outsmart them and listen instead."**

—Phil Argyris, Vice President, Transmission

Because of these exercises, BCD now has better scoping and definition of market needs. The EAB has given BCD confidence to make tough decisions regarding their R&D dollars. They are avoiding addressing individual workflows that can ultimately cost Harris and the customers more money. They've stopped second guessing what their customers need and trying to solve problems that don't need to be fixed. They are listening to their customers.

Customer Relationships

Harris BCD began their journey with a desire to develop deep relationships with customer executives who could help them better understand the market and provide insights that would drive increased satisfaction, sales, and retention. The team accomplished the relationship objectives with the *individuals* participating in the EAB, but not with the organizations participating in the EAB.

As the complexity of the solutions needed to serve global organizations was growing, it was clear Harris needed to move and align with the market from a sales perspective as well. Harris was viewed and delivered as a "reliable supplier" to their top customers. But it was clear that the top customers were looking for Harris to become more of a "problem solver" delivering solutions to their business issues.

Harris attacked this model on a test or pilot basis for three of the EAB accounts by forming an executive-sponsored account based innovation program (ABI). The executive sponsor program enabled the executive team member from Harris to connect directly with an executive member of the EAB. These two leaders would bring appropriate team members together to explore and more deeply understand the customers' operations and for the customer to better understand how BCD could solve their problems. These pilot ABI accounts provided the management team with the next layer of insight to recognize that media companies' needs are broader and more challenging than product-level functions.

> ### *"We're having better conversations internally as a team and with customers—understanding what their business problems are and how we align our teams to help solve them."*

–Harris Morris, President

Relationship Stages:

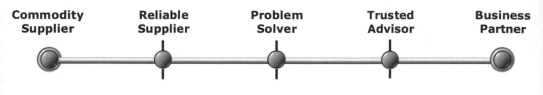

| Commodity Supplier | Reliable Supplier | Problem Solver | Trusted Advisor | Business Partner |

Harris select three marquee media accounts to work with. Each of these organizations came with different needs, requirements, and challenges.

The executive vice president for a major motion picture studio account brought in his team of vice presidents to openly meet with the BCD team. A full day of discussions and engagement led to a couple of clear insights for BCD. A tour of the studio facilities and operations led to the insight that they buy equipment from major hardware providers. Some of the equipment could be provided by Harris. It was also recognized that the customer was moving to 3D-generated content, and this new frontier could create a mutually beneficial opportunity for an industry leader like Harris and a partner for the motion picture studio.

The second account was a major cable provider, and the approach brought immediate recognition of key projects and account challenges to Harris Morris. Morris came away with the realization that the company needed to better organize around these key major accounts, that rapid and low-cost deployment of new TV channels is an emerging requirement, and that BCD has service-based opportunities that needed to be explored.

With a satellite broadcaster, BCD immediately identified a request for proposal (RFP) that had been issued, but BCD wasn't asked to respond to it. After quick and timely discussions, BCD was able to submit a large proposal in a matter of weeks.

By aligning themselves with these major accounts at an executive level, the BCD leadership team now has insight needed to position BCD to listen, learn, and lead the market. As a result of the program, Harris is looking to expand their account-management structure with savvy solution-oriented account managers to engage with customers in line with the approach used with these major accounts.

Global Expansion

Richard Scott, senior vice president of global sales and service recognized the impact the EAB was having on Harris and the relationships with major accounts. Richard needed relationships in Europe and Africa & Middle East and South Asia (EA&MESA) to define market needs, build brand awareness, and grow revenues.

The formation of the EA&MESA EAB came with a few more challenges than the America's EAB. In EA&MESA, Harris had two primary obstacles in their way toward creating and fostering relationships with major EA&MESA accounts. First, brand recognition of Harris BCD in EA&MESA was weak. In a recent independent market-based survey, Harris wasn't in the top 30 list of media company providers. Secondly, Harris primarily sold products in EA&MESA through third-party channels. These third-party channels owned the relationships with the EA&MESA customers, which meant that BCD would be starting from ground zero to build relationships to gain insight.

By leveraging the success of the Americas EAB, Richard Scott was able to engage the newly created EA&MESA sales force and recruit a solid group of 14 EA&MESA marquee accounts and thought leaders. An inaugural meeting led to creation of relationships between the EAB members and the Harris Executive team, and further clarified the focus on file-based workflows, interoperability, and alignment with the market. Harris BCD now has a global customer market-based perspective.

> *"The EAB has provided significant growth opportunities outside of individual lines of customer engagement. We've gone from providing a simple system to an enterprise-wide model. Neither of us could achieve it on our own, but together, we've developed something really special."*

–Richard Scott, SVP, Global Sales and Service

Summary Results

Since the customer-engagement program has such broad and deep implications to the company, Harris BCD measures results in a number of areas. From a financial perspective, the combined value of orders Harris received from EAB members' organizations represented 18.6 percent of the total value of orders received in North America in FY'09, up 3.1 percent from FY'08. Achieving a greater concentration of orders from the major media-company customers was crucial, given the industry consolidation occurring in the space. The division could not afford to be on the outside looking in with respect to making headway with the enterprise accounts.

More strategically, Harris is spending time with the right companies and individuals who have a vested interest in their future. They are giving them the guidance, confidence, and passion Harris needs to transform their business. These customers challenge their thinking and push them in new directions. The insights into the product portfolio and in aligning the company to the market are invaluable. Metrics in product development are difficult to place, but by avoiding development missteps, focusing on the right solutions, and delivering to major accounts, BCD is aligned for future success.

Intesource

INTESOURCE ENLISTS EXECUTIVE
CUSTOMERS TO DRIVE A TURNAROUND

*I*ntesource, Inc., was in a no-growth situation and losing money at an accelerating rate. Times were very difficult for this provider of procurement and sourcing solutions that lower the cost of goods and services purchased by its customers. All of this was happening in an industry that was in growth mode.

The CEO at Intesource, Inc., had an interesting business philosophy: "We will build what I think the customer wants and if they are smart, they will buy it…or it's their loss." The disastrous results of this approach included ballooning infrastructure costs and losses, no revenue growth, demoralized employees, alienated customers and limited decision-maker access, and a very dissatisfied board of directors.

"We were faced with two choices," recalls one member of the board, "close the company doors or give Tom Webster, our CMO, a chance to put Intesource back on a profitable growth course. Tom had proven himself in his current role, so we decided to give him his shot."

Webster was up for the challenge, and he believed that Intesource had a sound core: great customers, experienced and knowledgeable associates, and a model that could be successful. But among his biggest immediate challenges was gaining back customers' trust. While customers weren't bailing on Intesource, they were very unhappy with Webster's predecessor and the tone he had set. As a result, they didn't view Intesource as a strategic partner but rather as a vendor. They certainly had no desire to give Intesource any additional business, let alone recommend the company to other prospective buyers.

"They had a solid service and the support team was great," recalls a longstanding customer. "But I didn't feel the company's leadership was interested in hearing what I had to say. They thought they knew our business needs better than we did."

At this point, Intesource had about 35 customers, with the top six delivering more than 80 percent of revenue. Webster himself met face-to-face with the top 15 customers and via phone with the rest. His message: Intesource was committed to changing how it treated and engaged customers. In nearly every account, this approach repaired the damage and established enough trust and credibility to raise the relationship to the senior executive level.

Market Alignment

> ### "Having the market as the catalyst for our plans, priorities and resource allocation was a no-brainer."

—Tom Webster

To develop and deliver a sustainable vision and strategy at Intesource, Webster knew his company needed to play a more instrumental role in the growth of its customers. This is why moving the relationship up within the customer hierarchy was so important—Intesource had to get to the leaders in customer companies and understand what was important to them and why. "Having the market as the catalyst for our plans, priorities, and resource allocation was a no-brainer," says Webster. "Ultimately, the customer will only pay a premium for services that will move their business ahead. Aligning to these needs made gaining support, alignment, and excitement significantly easier to achieve with both my board (who funded the plan) and the employees (who executed the plan)."

Webster had seen before the success generated from bringing executive customers together in market collectives while with previous employers, so he decided to try it with Intesource's eight most strategic customers. He wanted to know how they viewed his company: what Intesource wasn't doing that it should be; and how it could help customers grow their businesses. "Whether a $10 million or a $10 billion company, the insight a group of true decision-makers delivers via a council is universal, and, in my experience, unmatched by any other approach," says Webster.

Internal Alignment

Internal alignment was another benefit Webster was hoping to capture by creating an executive customer advisory council. Intesource's leadership team was solid, but they were beaten down, unclear on direction, and fast losing their passion. They began to revive when Webster brought them together with the company's most important executive customers. Having the team listen, learn, understand, and probe customer needs and goals was a catalyst that rallied the Intesource team and united them in the task of figuring out how to design the solutions to address these customer requirements.

The council's input and direction delivered greater energy and focus for the Intesource team. "We listened, listened, and listened some more," Webster recalls. "They told us what their problems were, what we needed to address, how we needed to communicate with them … you name it."

> ## "We viewed and treated the council as an extension of our team."
>
> —Tom Webster

One of the customers' biggest issues was vetting new suppliers, and Intesource took on the challenge and developed a solution to address it. But the council's value went beyond product development. Its members weighed in on the company's marketing campaigns, support programs, and pricing models, too. On one occasion, the team presented a major marketing initiative. Yes, being a marketing person the majority of his career, Tom was very proud of the plan. Well, they hated it and said it wouldn't work. Of course, Tom still tested it … and the council was right, it didn't work. Tom shrugged his shoulders and jokingly admitted, "They were right, I was wrong, so we didn't roll it out. That saved us from wasting 20 percent of our annual marketing budget." Tom went on to say, "I swallowed my pride but was even more grateful for the savings."

Summarizing the executive customer advisory council initiative, Tom stated, "We viewed and treated them as an extension of our team. We opened the kimono to our firm ... the good, the bad, and the ugly. That was very hard, but the trust and relationship which was established was beyond description. They not only designed our next generation of solutions, marketing plans, customer support programs, and pricing models, they also helped design our future."

Intesource

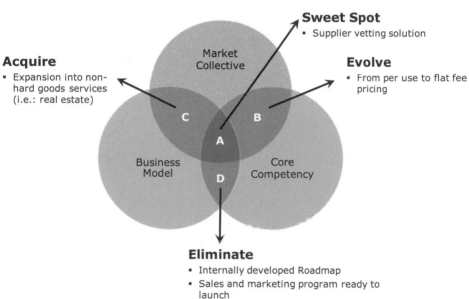

Sweet Spot
- Supplier vetting solution

Acquire
- Expansion into non-hard goods services (i.e.: real estate)

Market Collective

Evolve
- From per use to flat fee pricing

C

B

A

Business Model

D

Core Competency

Eliminate
- Internally developed Roadmap
- Sales and marketing program ready to launch

Predictable Revenue Growth

The financial results of Intesource's executive-customer initiative were impressive. Account growth among the eight customers leapt 100 percent. And many of them referred new prospects. In fact, one member referred and helped secure three new customers in a six-month timeframe.

In creating its council, Intesource also built a foundation for strategic relationships that ultimately resulted in business partnership, and these partnerships resulted in new opportunities, greater resistance to competitive threats, and loyal customers who ask, "What other kinds of things can you do for our company?"

Today in nearly every top account, Intesource has established relationships with multiple members of the C-suite, including CFOs and CEOs. Being under $50 million, and with the average size of these customers at more than $3 billion, these relationships are something Intesource's leadership team is very proud of and holds dear.

These relationships have helped Intesource in many ways. In one case, an executive at one of Intesource's biggest customers brought in a large consulting group for a project, which recommended replacing Intesource with another firm. "When our executive sponsors realized what was happening, they made sure the contract with Intesource was renewed early," says Webster. "If the same situation had occurred two years earlier, we would have lost a seven-figure deal and not even known why or how."

With the help of major customers, Webster successfully developed a long-term vision and plan for Intesource. "Ultimately, these interactions gave me and the team the clarity and confidence to put a stake in the ground," he says. It was a tall stake: Intesource's leadership team planned to profitably double the top line in three years, double the customer base, and develop a new offering that provided more business value than anything in the current portfolio.

Despite coming from an entirely different industry, Tom had now gained the respect of his team and his customers. Tom was still an unknown entity with respect to running the entire firm. He successfully cleared the first hurdle in setting the vision and delivering a strategic plan the board and leadership teams believed in. Now the second phase, successful execution of the plan, lay ahead. To continue to distance himself from the former CEO, who had originally hired him, Tom now had to focus on performance.

Create Customer Advocates

Since then, Intesource has turned to its council at key points to make sure the company remains aligned to customers' needs from both a user and business perspective. It has also turned to the council for sales assistance. "We needed more prospects to hear our story to meet our revenue goals," says Webster.

Once Intesource won over its existing customers, it created a summit in which its customers could gather with their peers to discuss issues and share experiences, best practices, and lessons learned.

Those who attended the Summit showed a close rate 300 percent higher than those who didn't attend.

The eight advisory council members are active participants in Intesource's summit, "Innovation Summit: Best Practices in e-Sourcing and Procurement." Customers actually present and lead the conference. Customers own the content, topics, and agenda. Intesource simply helps organize and facilitate the meeting. The success of this annual conference is a direct result of the relationships and genuine belief in the Intesource process and new company culture. This summit generated a buzz in the industry for Intesource.

The market buzz created by the summit enhanced Intesource's deal flow, deal size, and new customer acquisition rate. By having Intesource customers talk about their solutions, it was exponentially more credible than if Intesource presented. It was so real in content and a huge deal-flow accelerator. Those who attended this conference showed a close rate 300 percent higher than those who didn't. Time-to-close for this group was nearly cut in half as well, which was great for Intesource's cash flow. Intesource worked extremely hard on earning the relationships with current customers, and the summit, like the council, had to be beneficial for them as well. With the right formula, this approach gave Intesource the vehicle to meet their aggressive growth goals.

This summit had another long-term benefit for Intesource. "Since it is led by customers, we continue to get educated and smarter about how their industry is changing and what we should be thinking about, addressing with them and developing for them," Webster says. "This educates and upgrades our entire staff. It challenges our thinking. It impacts our strategy development, marketing, sales, and customer service."

The Bottom Line

Ultimately the combination and integration of top-account meetings, the council, and the summit enabled Intesource to form a more symbiotic relationship with the market. In the short term, Intesource listened and created a new strategic plan. The company worked the plan and leveraged the market insights it gained to build more valuable solutions. It also leveraged the relationship, trust, and credibility by having their customers share their experiences in working with Intesource. The results:

- The customer base grew from 35 to 60 customers
- Revenue doubled in three years
- The company transformed red ink into profitable growth
- Twelve customers deliver 80 percent of revenues vs. six customers three years ago
- Customer-satisfaction levels are the highest in its industry

Intesource's culture, balance sheet, and income statement are vastly different from three years ago when the board almost closed the company. The investors are thrilled with the financial progress and results that have been attained under Webster's leadership.

SPRINGER TAPS EXECUTIVE CUSTOMERS FOR STRATEGIC TRANSFORMATION

"In 2004, we had an arm's-length relationship with our customers . . ."

"There was no need for interaction," recalls Syed Hasan, Springer's president of Global STM Academic Sales.

Springer, the world's second-largest publisher of journals in the STM (Science, Technology, Medicine) sector and the largest publisher of STM books, like other publishers at the time was selling journals through subscription agents and books through trade book sellers. Orders were simply passed from agents to publishers.

Prior to 2000, the publishing industry was largely static. Content distribution hadn't changed much since 1436 when Gutenberg invented the printing press. But … the introduction of electronic document formats combined with broad-based Internet adoption was about to dramatically change this laid-back industry. Much like the music industry just a few years before, new content formats, electronic distribution, and easily accessible content through the presence of Google were creating radical shifts in the roles of readers, authors, librarians, and, of course, publishers.

Springer Science+Business Media's strategy needed to change. CEO Derk Haank knew that the emergence of revolutionary digital and electronic technologies would transform the publishing industry. But he also knew that, without solid guidance from the publisher's core library customers, transformative strategic change entailed betting-the-business-sized risk.

Springer had very little interaction with its customers to that point. According to Syed Hasan, the company had only one employee who worked directly with librarians, and most of its sales were transacted through third parties.

Then, a few things began to come together …

Setting the Stage for Strategic Market Insight

In 2004, at the same time digital publishing began to accelerate, Springer merged with Kluwer Academic Publishers. As the two companies became one, and the idea of an e-content business model became more and more compelling, there was a tremendous amount of uncertainty within the company. "We needed to get validation on our strategy and feedback on product development much earlier in the lifecycle," recalls Hasan. "Not only did we need quicker time to market, we needed to have immediate product acceptance."

That's when Springer decided to form its executive customer advisory board. Its members included decision-making head librarians and the leaders of buying consortia.

The initial meetings were a bit rough. "The publishing side of the house had interest in talking with customers, but only about content they were interested in having us get for them. We needed to address content distribution and business models," recalls Hasan. "We also started out with a lot of lectures … us talking and using PowerPoint slides. Our CEO was present, and he and other executives didn't find much value in the presentations. The customers also told us the sessions were too long and they weren't gaining much value."

The team took this input to heart. The format of the meetings was changed, and the company adopted a new approach designed to drive dialogue and hear from their customers.

It worked. "Validating Springer's vision through input from our key customers was a fundamental change. It enabled us to gain acceptance from the marketplace at an early stage and fueled our growth, allowing us to soar past the competition," says Hasan.

> ## *"Based on our customer-engagement strategy, we were several years ahead of competitors."*

—Syed Hasan, President of Global STM Academic Sales

Advancing the Model

Recognizing that gaining market insight and building relationships in a single market was not enough to win globally, Springer quickly built a library advisory board model that could be rolled out globally, in a successful effort to cover the company's key geographies and markets. "As a global publisher we need to listen to our customers on a global basis," says Juliane Ritt, executive vice president of global marketing. "We must have customer engagement programs in place that will support our e-First strategies."

Over several years, Springer built a global program that supports regional and industry vertical markets to gain market insight and drive growth, including:

- Academic Market (Springer's largest market)
- Americas Library Advisory Board
- ROW (Rest of World) Library Advisory Board
- ASIA Academic Library Advisory Board
- Middle East/Northern Africa Library Advisory Board
- Latin America Library Advisory Board
- Global Corporate Library Advisory Board
- Government Library Advisory Board

The main objectives of the program are to gain market insight and foster stronger executive-customer relationships. The annual advisory board meetings are typically attended by 16 to 20 customers, although some meetings have had as many as 30. The meetings are interactive and focused on strategy, product and service innovation, and business model creation/modifications.

The company's rate of innovation has dramatically increased since it began soliciting customer input. "We have made great strides in the last six years," Hasan notes. "We have been tremendously successful with new products and services, and we can directly attribute that success to the direction we were given by our advisory boards."

To foster this trend, beginning in late 2009, many of the advisory board meetings included innovation as a formal agenda item. Advisory board members participate in workshops where they are asked to develop and design a new product, build its business model, plan the go-to-market strategy, and present the concept to a broader audience.

"This exercise was tough. It stretched us and gave us a whole new appreciation for what Springer goes through when developing new products," said board member Joe Gerrard. "They take a lot of time to understand our world, so it is great to have a chance to get a glimpse into theirs."

Organizational Alignment

The transition from traditional print publishing to electronic publishing was not necessarily an easy concept for the executive team to sell internally. "There was tremendous opposition from our own publishing group to allow books to be made electronically," recalls Hasan. "But our CEO, Derk Haank, led the charge. He saw an opportunity to take our huge market share in books and make it more profitable by digitizing our content."

Advisory boards proved an invaluable resource as Springer moved into uncharted territory. And their members were very clear on what would work and what wouldn't.

"We really listened to them. They said 'no' to digital rights management. They wanted to own the electronic content rather than rent it. They wanted to only pay once, and the list goes on and on," Hasan says. "As a result, we are the only publisher with this model, and it has been very profitable for us."

Having the internal team in the room to hear this market input directly helped bring the alignment that was critical to Springer's progress. "I have personally engaged with these customers and heard directly from them. The input we receive is critical and has provided an opportunity for us to achieve greater profitability in a shorter amount of time than it would have taken without their direction," says Peter Hendricks, president of publishing.

Today, board-member insight is being used by Springer executives to gain support internally for new projects. "Having pre-validated ideas helps accelerate acceptance within Springer, and that, in turn, helps us go to market faster," says Hasan. "Beating out the competition is a direct result of getting market insight at a very early stage."

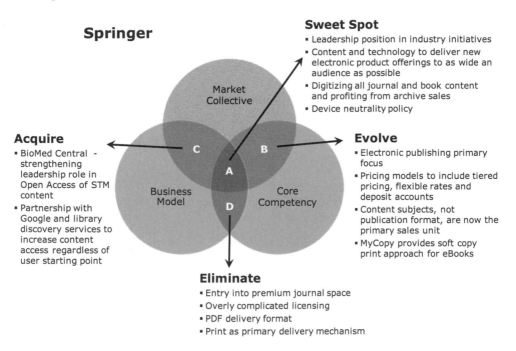

Springer

Sweet Spot
- Leadership position in industry initiatives
- Content and technology to deliver new electronic product offerings to as wide an audience as possible
- Digitizing all journal and book content and profiting from archive sales
- Device neutrality policy

Market Collective

Acquire
- BioMed Central - strengthening leadership role in Open Access of STM content
- Partnership with Google and library discovery services to increase content access regardless of user starting point

C   B
A
Business Model   Core Competency
D

Evolve
- Electronic publishing primary focus
- Pricing models to include tiered pricing, flexible rates and deposit accounts
- Content subjects, not publication format, are now the primary sales unit
- MyCopy provides soft copy print approach for eBooks

Eliminate
- Entry into premium journal space
- Overly complicated licensing
- PDF delivery format
- Print as primary delivery mechanism

Customer Retention and Advocacy

Springer's executive-customer programs have enabled them to build better customer relationships and enhance engagement levels. "I find tremendous value from these advisory boards, not just for the great business insights they provide, but also through the social time that is built into the agendas where we are able to engage with our customers more informally. That leads to stronger relationships," says CEO Derk Haank.

And revenue tracking supports the value. "The stronger relationships have led to a 10 percent increase in contracted revenue with accounts that participate in the library advisory board program versus those that do not," reports George Scotti, marketing vice president.

But Springer executives are quick to point out that advisory boards are not intended to be direct sales vehicles. "We really don't use it as a sales opportunity," says Hasan. "We need our customers to feel like they benefit by coming to these engagements so they will continue to participate. The last thing you want is for customers to feel like we wasted their time."

In addition to the advisory boards, Springer recently launched an eBook summit series for customers and prospects. These summits, which include face-to-face meetings and virtual meetings conducted via the Internet, are meant to position Springer as a thought leader, drive awareness, and generate leads. Existing customers tell their stories to a much broader audience, and then the participants have an opportunity to network and discuss industry challenges together.

Because Springer has developed such strong relationships with the advisory board members, they can now leverage those relationships at the summits. "We encourage them to speak openly about their successes with Springer as well as their challenges," says Hasan. "The audience knows we really want to help solve their business issues, and the benefits of having a third party illustrate that through open dialogue is significant."

A recent Latin American Council had an amazing 100 percent of members volunteering to participate in one or more advocate-based activities.

Hasan shared that having their customers become advocates is the natural iteration for Springer through their journey, and they now have an extensive database of customers who have volunteered to do the following:

- Participate in a case study

- Sit on a panel at select events

- Publish articles in the Springer newsletter

- Co-author white papers

- Speak at an event

- Talk with peers about Springer (as a reference)

In addition to the benefits of building relationships and having customers speak on their behalf, Springer can also point to the bottom-line impact of the summits. In a summit recently held in New York, 100 percent of the participants said they would recommend the summit to a peer; 48 percent of attendees previously identified as prospects became leads; and of those, 64 percent signed a deal with Springer generating a 41 percent increase in revenue from the participant group.

Bringing It All Together

Hasan says that the advisory council meetings as well as the eBooks summits have gotten the attention of the board of directors, and now the board members are regularly updated on the feedback coming directly from the market via these initiatives.

You won't find many organizations with a more dedicated long-term commitment to gaining customer insights than Springer. The reason for the commitment: they know and understand the profound impact it has on accelerating growth.

"We know the value we get from executive-customer programs, so they are now a major part of our business strategy," says Hasan. "We are able to completely close the loop with the insights we get from our advisory board members and summit participants, and at the end of the day, they make us more profitable. And ultimately, isn't that why anyone is in business?"

WELL FARGO GOES FROM FOCUS GROUPS TO CUSTOMER FOCUS

Where do you find competitive advantage when your core offering appears to be a commodity? For Wells Fargo, a diversified financial services company with more than $1.3 trillion assets under management, it comes from understanding customers better than anyone else, and fulfilling their needs in unparalleled and innovative ways.

"We want to satisfy all of our customers' financial needs, help them succeed financially, be the premier provider of financial services in every one of our markets, and be known as one of America's great companies," says chairman and CEO John G. Stumpf. "Getting there requires a total focus on the customer, partnering as One Wells Fargo [imagining ourselves as the customer] to earn 100 percent of every customer's business."

For a company with such lofty goals, you'd assume Wells Fargo was customer focused from day one. Instead, it's been an evolution.

A key inflection point came in the late 1990s, when the emergence of the Internet led Wells Fargo to wonder how it could help them build stronger relationships in the B2B space. Steve Ellis, executive vice president, wholesale banking, provided the answer with his vision for commercial Internet banking. Dick Kovacevich, chairman at the time, liked the idea and asked Ellis to head up a new group, Wholesale Internet Solutions, with the purpose of developing online services for commercial customers.

> *"An important part of this process was understanding what this could mean for our customers. Could it help them do things faster, simpler, or smarter?"*

—Steve Ellis, EVP, Wholesale Banking, Wells Fargo

The first major project was an online portal for commercial banking customers. That was the beginning of CEO, the Commercial Electronic Office® portal. Wells Fargo knew it couldn't develop the portal in a vacuum. "An important part of this process was understanding what this could mean for our customers," remembers Ellis. "Could it help them do things faster, simpler, or smarter?"

Wells Fargo needed to engage a group of customers to view the portal and provide feedback, but at that time customer engagement was more a concept than a reality. "It wasn't a concept most businesses were talking about," says Jeff Tinker, senior vice president, treasury management wholesale market product strategy. "We gave a lot of thought to who we should talk to, and, in fairness, who would want to talk to us?"

Tinker's team went out to the relationship teams across the bank and asked them which commercial customers might provide the best feedback. This led the team to many of their most vocal and opinionated customers.

The customer feedback group, or advisory council as it became known, was purposely kept small. It included 12 customers who met in person twice a year with senior bank executives. The group was diverse; representation spanned industries, titles, spend, and experiences with technology.

[*"It really took us by surprise how much
the customers interacted. In the end, we
realized the value in the forum we had created."*]

Jeff Tinker, SVP, Treasury Management Product Strategy, Wells Fargo

One of them was Kim Hansen, cash manager for Orange County, California. She recalls how impressed she was with the changes that resulted from her group's feedback. "It wasn't everyone sitting around patting Wells Fargo on the back," says Hansen. "They are a big organization and have your typical issues. The difference is they were there to find out the pain points and work through them."

"We initially started out with a product focus and really thought the council would be more like a super focus group," recalls Tinker. "It really took us by surprise how much the customers talked amongst themselves. We realized the value in the forum was more than we expected. We were able to get feedback from clients, and they walked away from the meeting feeling like they had gotten more than they had given."

Tinker and fellow executives were also surprised by the bonds that developed among council participants. "One of the original council members was from a large national retailer, and during the spring meeting, she said, 'I feel like you guys are family and I want to invite you all to my wedding in the fall,'" relates Tinker. "My boss at the time asked, 'Where are you getting married?' and she said Chicago. He said, 'So we should have the fall council meeting in Chicago.' And we did. All of the council members were in attendance—at both the meeting and the wedding!"

> ## *"Our customers told us,*
> ## *"There's nothing like this.'*

—Jeff Tinker

Given the quality of council's feedback and the powerful customer relationships it engendered, Wells Fargo decided to do advisory councils more formally and more broadly—growing from one advisory council to three.

As Wells Fargo started to expand its councils, it sought members from companies in more diverse geographies and industries. "We looked at size and considered adding prospects to the councils," says Tinker. "We added two middle-market councils and one small-business group council. In 2003 there were five councils; in 2011, it was twelve."

Executive Advisory Board Objectives		
Customer Engagement	**Strategy and Trends**	**Offerings**
• Identify, **build, and foster relationships** with market-leading organizations. • Understand processes, practices, and methods to **accelerate sales** in target accounts.	• **Identify emerging trends** and determine the timing, impact, potential business models, and operational changes necessary to succeed. • Understand where and **how to allocate resources** for success in the market.	• Understand the Harris **value proposition** to achieve greater penetration of end-to-end solutions. • **Identify future portfolio improvements** and innovations. • **Understand solution adoption** timing and impact.

While twelve councils may seem like a lot to manage, Wells Fargo is convinced of their value. "The advisory councils are critical to validate where we are going and what we are doing," declares Tinker. They have been a key component to Wells Fargo's innovation, helping the bank adjust its strategy in relation to market and technological shifts.

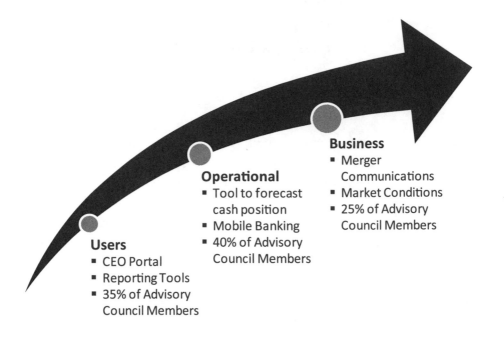

Users
- CEO Portal
- Reporting Tools
- 35% of Advisory Council Members

Operational
- Tool to forecast cash position
- Mobile Banking
- 40% of Advisory Council Members

Business
- Merger Communications
- Market Conditions
- 25% of Advisory Council Members

For example, wholesale mobile banking was vetted by the council. The one watershed moment came at a meeting in Denver. The treasurer of a large restaurant needed to approve a large wire transfer, but he didn't have his PC with him. He was in a sheer panic because by the time he made it back to his office he would have missed the window. In the end, Wells Fargo was able to help him. When he was finished approving the wire, he approached the group of bankers, all using their BlackBerries and said, "I need to be able to do what I just did on one of these," and he pointed to a BlackBerry. Wells took that feedback, did additional research in council meetings and with the user-experience team before launching CEO Mobile—and all well ahead of the competition.

In other instances, the value of the Advisory Council was not that it agreed with Wells Fargo's proposed business concept, but that they said 'no.' At one point Wells thought about getting into the accounting business—delivering services via their CEO Portal. They'd seen how successful Quicken and QuickBooks had been and figured we they would do the same. However, when vetted with the council, they told Wells, "You might be able to deliver it, but that is not your core competency. We want you to focus on being even better at banking, not expanding into some new business line so you can make more money." They took it a step farther and told Wells what would really help would be to make it easier to integrate their accounting packages directly with the bank. Tinker added, "So, in addition to hearing 'No,' we got a great suggestion on how we could add value for our customers."

Feedback from the various advisory councils has also led to improvements in reporting and how customers access the portal. "We had a wakeup call for our portal product team, when one of our council members told us how he wished he could spend *less* time on the portal," says Tinker. The product team took the feedback and turned it into event messaging—email notifications that could tell the customer when something important was awaiting their attention on the portal.

"I've never really seen another bank do this," says council member Bryan Wilson, Wind River's vice president in charge of corporate treasury. "They ask a lot of questions, but do a greater amount of listening. I could go in there with something unexpected and they would take it and run with it. I told them we wanted to make all of our payments electronically. They said, 'You know, that's not a bad idea,' and rolled out a product a couple of months later."

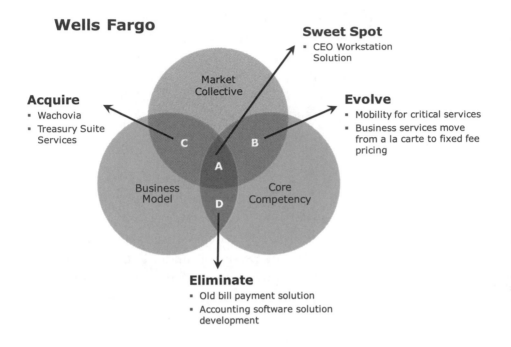

Wells Fargo

Sweet Spot
- CEO Workstation Solution

Market Collective

Acquire
- Wachovia
- Treasury Suite Services

Evolve
- Mobility for critical services
- Business services move from a la carte to fixed fee pricing

C

B

A

Business Model

Core Competency

D

Eliminate
- Old bill payment solution
- Accounting software solution development

Advisory councils have become so critical in Wells Fargo's development and strategic planning process that Tinker says internally people have started asking, "Hey, have we engaged our council?"

Advisory group members provide input that goes far beyond products. "In one case, they said some of our sales people feel like order takers," says Tinker. "That's not product feedback. That kind of feedback involves a lot of different groups. But it is incredibly valuable for us to hear."

> *"They win more business not because we look the other way on price or service, but because they understand us better."*

—Jon Wells, Director, Treasury and Planning at Allstate

Council input can also affect operational costs. When Wells Fargo was planning to relocate Allstate's relationship manager nearer to the insurer's headquarters, council member Jon Wells, director of treasury and planning at Allstate, told the bank the move was unnecessary. "We were able to tell them that our relationship officer does not have to be local," recalls Wells. "We need an effective thought leader who understands our business, but we don't care if they are in New York or California."

Customer engagement is so important at Wells Fargo that Tinker can't imagine how other companies operate without advisory councils. "Frankly, I struggle to understand how any company can be successful today without actively engaging its customers," he says. "It's kind of like playing darts blindfolded. You may get lucky, but chances are good you'll have far more failures—especially if your competition is not wearing a blindfold."

Wells Fargo doesn't leave its success to chance. In fact, advisory councils are just one core component for gathering feedback. They also employ ethnography studies, user-experience teams, and social media. All customer input is reviewed quarterly, prioritized, and assigned an owner who ensures action is taken and customers know it.

And the results justify the investment. Advisory council members have higher retention rates than non-participating customers. They also do more business with the bank. "They win more business," says Jon Wells, "not because we look the other way on price or service, but because they understand us better, and they know how to bid it and service it better."

The relationships developed through Wells Fargo's councils have produced loyal customer advocates. "We often videotape council members to use in our marketing," says Tinker. In one instance, a council member asked Wells Fargo to present with him at a national conference.

The bank's status as a trusted partner with its largest customers has also been invaluable as Wells Fargo and Wachovia embark on the largest bank merger in history. Councils helped Wells Fargo develop their communication strategy for the merger. "We were discussing key merger-related decisions we thought we had communicated to our customers when a council member raised his hand and said, 'I haven't heard about any of these decisions.' Then additional hands started going up around the table," says Tinker. "Uh oh, we realized we had a problem. These were our best customers and they were not receiving our communication."

In response, the bank engaged council members to identify a multi-pronged strategy that included direct communication to customers, utilizing both the Web and email, and personal messaging delivered by the bank's sales officers and relationship managers.

Customer engagement has helped Wells Fargo's stock price rise 20 times over the past 25 years. In addition, the bank has been named not only one of the world's most admired companies, but also one of the world's most respected companies.

"I know without a doubt we are one of the world's most respected companies because of our advisory councils and other customer-focused programs—because of our total commitment to the customer," states Tinker. "It goes well beyond lip service. Our commitment to the customer is a corporate objective. If you share, listen, and act on your customers' needs and desires, they will drive your success with sustainable and predictable, profitable growth."

Thinking of Starting an Advisory Council?

Advice from Jeff Tinker, SVP, Treasury Management Wholesale Market Product Strategy, Wells Fargo

1. **Don't be afraid to ask customers what they want.** When we first started there was a fear of asking customers what they wanted because we didn't want to hear negative feedback about our people, pricing, etc. Then we realized this was exactly what we needed to hear, and it was a great forum in which to discuss.

2. **If you really want to engage customers—mean it!** Don't give lip service to the word "customer." Think of all the surveys you've participated in over your lifetime. How many times do we ever find out what someone did with the information? Customers need to know your plan.

3. **Stick to "must knows."** Before each council meeting we start out with 20 pages of questions and pare it back to 2. What are the most important questions? What must you know versus what is nice to know?

4. **What's in it for me (WIIFM)?** Consider the customer. What do they want to hear their peers talk about? With each RSVP we ask council members to share agenda topics of interest and importance to them.

"THE ENEMY OF GREAT IS GOOD ..."

… especially in the case of Crown Partners. After five years in business, they had a solid track record. They consistently showed profitable and steady growth. Every product they made was sold before the first hour of labor was accounted for. And CEO Richard Hearn was able to assemble a strong team of smart, talented people.

So why isn't this great?

For starters, Hearn realized that this was not a sustainable model. In year five, Hearn recognized that while their products were successful, they had too many of them and there were no synergies between them.

"Every product we built was a success, because we didn't build anything unless we knew we were going to sell it," Hearn says. "But I knew we missed some big opportunities by thinking this way."

For Hearn, the time had come to develop a broader strategy if they wanted to continue their exponential growth. "We were sharing a grape and were content, but I felt there was something much bigger and I didn't know what it was or where to find it."

To satisfy this hunger and become great, something major had to change, according to Hearn. It was no longer good enough to provide quality products and services to Crown Partners' customers on a one-off basis. He had to find a way to evolve Crown Partners in a way that provided their customers with solutions that would be transformational to their respective businesses as well.

Organizational Alignment

That was a pretty tall order for an entrepreneur like Hearn, since following this logic would require him to say "no thanks" to customers ready and willing to pay for what Crown Partners could readily provide.

"We had to sharpen our vision. We not only had to decide what was working, but also what would work for the long-term," Hearn explains. "And that would require aligning our internal team first before we could move forward."

The first step toward aligning the Crown Partners team was to come to an agreement on what the market was demanding. "One of our employees suggested that we should conduct a forum with our customers to discuss our product and service offerings," Hearn said. "To be honest, I was very skeptical. I thought it would evolve into nothing more than a bitch-fest."

In fact, it confirmed for Hearn his team was in dire need of alignment, and the customers could bring that to fruition.

"It was completely surprising" according to Hearn, "Our engineers, product managers, and sales and marketing people all had varying ideas of what our customers wanted. Not everyone could be right, and ultimately, the customer knows more than any one of us internally." Hearn added that when your customers tell you what they want, it's very hard to argue with.

Innovation

This customer insight led to a new innovation that blew the doors off their current market. With the development of a solution (or better said, a "Program") suggested by a customer at the forum, Crown Partners was able to take a $10-million market and turn it into a $10-billion market, thus creating the first step in the exponential growth Hearn was starving for. "They, in fact, told us where the watermelon was."

What was becoming clear to Hearn was that this kind of vision and insight doesn't come from the users of their products and services, but rather from the influencers and, more strategically, from the decision makers.

"We chose to align to our customers' strategies, and it changed the game in a big way ... moving us from chasing grapes to catching watermelons."

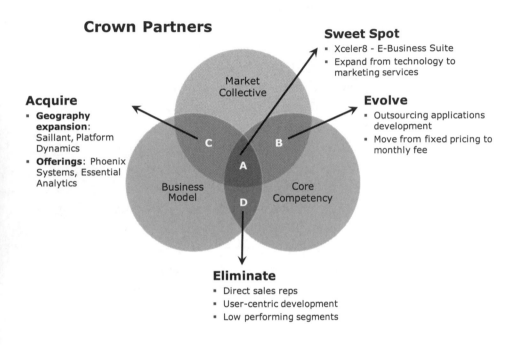

Crown Partners

Sweet Spot
- Xceler8 - E-Business Suite
- Expand from technology to marketing services

Market Collective

Acquire
- **Geography expansion**: Saillant, Platform Dynamics
- **Offerings**: Phoenix Systems, Essential Analytics

Evolve
- Outsourcing applications development
- Move from fixed pricing to monthly fee

C

B

A

Business Model

D

Core Competency

Eliminate
- Direct sales reps
- User-centric development
- Low performing segments

Market Alignment

"We had to move past thinking feature/function. We needed to partner with the executives of targeted customers to help solve their business issues if we were going to accomplish our goals of sustainability, profitability, and growth," Hearn explains. To do that, Hearn knew he had to find the right customers at the right level for whom Crown Partners could make giant leaps.

Identifying those targets meant developing an accurate profile and forging relationships at the highest levels in order to engage in meaningful dialogue with the people at the top. "We had to let our customers be the catalyst for change. This is not a hobby; it's a business and we must add value to our customers in a way that makes money. The only way to do that is to listen to the people running the companies."

Bringing it All Together

As a direct result of aligning their leadership team, aligning their offerings to the market, focusing on innovation that solves business issues, and subsequently creating customer advocates, Crown Partners more than doubled their sales over the next three years (greater than two times their industry). Additionally, they have increased their customer base by 400 percent and have 80 percent of their revenue represented by 20 percent of their customers. The culmination of their success is wrapped up in Crown Partners being named to a fifth straight *Inc* 500/5000 fastest-growing companies in America member—an accomplishment that only 50 other companies out of more than 25,000 have achieved.

"We aren't where we want to be yet, but we are heading in the right direction. We've found the watermelon, which is much bigger than the grape, but we only earned a couple of slices so far," Hearn concludes. "By focusing on the decision makers, aligning to their strategies and engaging in continuous dialogue at the highest levels, we will certainly continue moving forward at a rapid pace. Without it, we would have missed these opportunities and not even known it."

They didn't realize what they had left on the table, because they weren't at the table having the conversations with right people. For years, they didn't even recognize this … yes, the enemy of great is good.

INDEX

ACKNOWLEDGMENTS

So many people contributed to making this book happen. I hope I haven't left anyone out.

The B2B Playbook

Many have been attached to this project, but these anchors guided me on an ongoing basis the last two years:

Suzanne Smith: Continuous support on content, flow, and structure throughout the entire two years

Karen Battist: PR, Utility Player

Karen Penney: Graphics, grammar, and the patience of Job

Ted Kinni: Editor

Betsy Westhafer: Editing and grammar

Jayme Johnson: Publicity

Richard Hunt: Publisher

Geehan Team

I started on this journey more than two years ago, and the Geehan team has been supportive every step of the way editing, interviewing, writing case studies, etc.:

Karen Battist	Suzanne Smith
Kelly Jones	Amy Spahn
Laura Pardo	Misty Strawser
Karen Penney	Rob Urbanowicz
Karen Posey	Betsy Westhafer
Rachelle Smith	Phyllis Winters

Financial Research

The AllianceBernstein Global Wealth Management team is simply incredible. They added so much insight into developing the financial aspect of some of my key models . . . a level of depth that adds more value and proof to the stories shared.

> Eric Garfunkel, VP, Senior Research Associate
>
> Philip Kessler, VP, Financial Advisor
>
> A.M. (Toni) Sacconaghi, Jr., SVP, Senior Research Analyst,
>   IT Hardware

The Reviewers

These outside professionals took the time to review my "very rough" drafts with the utmost commitment and candid feedback. Many actually reviewed multiple times (* denotes multiple reviews). Thank you so much with your most generous gifts...time, support, and expert insight.

Tom Baird	Richard Hearn *
Doug Collins	Dan Knowles
Kurt Cumming	Scott Lomond *
Jerry Doubler	Doug Lunne
Chris Eifert	Mark O'Bryan
Rob Franks	Laura Ramos
Paul Friga	Pavani Reddy
Tom Gilman	Dave Sullivan
Jim Haudan	David Thomson *
Keith Hawk*	Eric Wagner

Case Studies and Key Content Contributors

Samir Bagga	Kathryn Kendall
Lisa Campbell	Shami Khorana
Krishnan Chatterjee	Harris Morris
Doug Collins	George Scotti
Scott Collins	Gowri Shankar Vembu
Jeb Dasteel	Tim Thorsteinson
Paul Dunay	Jeff Tinker
Syed Hasan	Brad Turner
Richard Hearn	Tom Webster

Mentors, Advisors, Influencers, and Friends

Brent Ahrens	Bob Hochwalt	Laura Ramos
Heike Auerbach	Mark Hurd	Anubhav Saxena
Jim Bolen	Pete Luongo	John Schwarz
Ellen Campbell-Kaminski	Dan Maher	Debashish Sinha
Molly Chillinsky	Clay Mathile	Gary Slack
Rob Connelly	John Matson	Dave Sullivan
Vicki Cooney	Katherine Miles	David Thomson
Jeff Garrity	Vail Miller, Jr.	Granville "Granny" Toogood
Paulette Gift	Joe Morgan	John Warren
Art Harlan	Dave Munn	Lloyd "Buzz" Waterhouse
Jim Haudan	Ralph Oliva	Lew Watts
Sami Hero	Kim Powell	

Family

Finally, without the support, patience and love from home, this book would not have been possible. Stephanie, Grace, Sarah, Mick, and Annie. . . .You are all the best, and I love you so much!